BARK B

▶▶▶▶▶▶▶▶▶▶▶▶▶▶▶▶▶▶▶▶▶▶

To Ancroft Animal
Rescue Kennels

Best Wishes

Sylvia Wilson
author

Lily of the Valley

This book is dedicated to my loving mother, Lillian Richards, who is now with God. This wonderful woman always believed in me, and her natural love of animals and children was, no doubt, inherited by me.

The day has come that I regret.
That was the day I'll never forget.
I'll miss you more than I can bear,
but in my heart you will always be there,
my lily of the valley.

BARK BUSTERS

▶ ▶ ▶ ▶ ▶ ▶ ▶ ▶ ▶ ▶ ▶ ▶ ▶ ▶ ▶ ▶ ▶ ▶ ▶ ▶

*How to solve your dog's everyday
behavioural problems*

Sylvia Wilson

SIMON & SCHUSTER
AUSTRALIA

BARK BUSTERS: HOW TO SOLVE YOUR DOG'S EVERYDAY
BEHAVIOURAL PROBLEMS

First published in Australia in 1993 by
Simon & Schuster Australia
20 Barcoo Street, East Roseville NSW 2069

Reprinted 1994

A Paramount Communications Company
Sydney New York London Toronto Tokyo Singapore

© Sylvia Wilson 1993

National Library of Australia
Cataloguing in Publication data

Wilson, Sylvia.
  Bark busters: how to solve your dog's behavioural
  problems.

  Includes index.
  ISBN 0 7318 0315 9.

  1. Dogs – Training. 2. Dogs – Behaviour. I. Title.

636.70887

Cover photograph of Lucy Townsend by Peter Solness
Illustrations by Michael White
Designed by Michelle Havenstein
Typeset in Australia by Asset Typesetting Pty Ltd
Printed in Australia by McPherson's Printing Group

We fell for the television advertisements. You know, the one with the Labrador puppy, selling toilet paper. We bought the Labrador pup — cute, bouncy and just a little bit naughty. We called her Lucy.

Six months later, she'd grown to twenty kilos of bounce. She wasn't cute. Lucy was a juvenile delinquent.

She dug enormous holes in the garden. She ate two TV remote controls. She raided the garbage and bailed up our friends.

'It's your dog ... I never wanted a dog ... you promised you'd train her.'

Then came the phone.

'Telecom'

'You may find this hard to believe, but our dog ate the phone ...'

'Labrador?'

'Yes, but ...'

'We'll send a technician.'

We called in Bark Busters. I expected a platoon dressed in full metal jackets, armed with rubber bullets. Sylvia wore high heels and a houndstooth suit. She spoke briefly to Lucy who realised she was outclassed and lay obediently at Sylvia's feet. Sylvia told us the facts of life. We were people. Lucy was a dog. Dogs need manners. Training a dog isn't cruel. The dog doesn't speak English. All those things and more, you'll learn in this book.

Sylvia showed us the simple, practical steps to good doggie manners. She demonstrated the magic word 'Bah', and a few other tricks.

These days, we are the people and Lucy is the dog. A calm, sensible, well-mannered dog. A dog that is a pleasure to have. That's what this book will give you too.

HELEN TOWNSEND

▶ ACKNOWLEDGEMENTS ◀

It is difficult to thank all the people without whose help and support this book might not have been possible. The list is long, but I have decided to thank them all. This book was made possible because of their combined help and their faith in me as a capable dog trainer.

To my husband, Danny, whose love, support and never-ending faith in me made this book possible. The wind beneath my wings.

To my parents, Eddie and Lily Richards (Lillian, God rest her soul), who put up with a precocious child who continually brought strays home. They always believed one day I would be a famous dog-trainer.

To my brother, John, who gave me so much help in the early days and gave me a greater knowledge of the psychology of people and animals and that magical word 'Bah'.

To my children, Brett and Donna, who have, without much reward, assisted me over the years and who will hopefully one day carry on the Bark Busters training techniques themselves.

To my dear departed friend, Jean Higgenbottom, an expert in her own right, who truly believed in me and contributed so much to my career. I have no doubt that Jean is here by my side assisting my every paragraph. Thanks, Jean, you are not forgotten.

To the RSPCA for giving me the opportunity to work with so many great dogs during my nine and a half years in charge of the South Coast NSW Branch. My years with them gave me an invaluable insight into dogs' behaviour and the ability to perfect my techniques.

To my friend, Doug Malouf, who long ago planted the seed when he said 'Sylvia, you must write a book'. Thanks, Doug, for all your help.

To author Helen Townsend, who very kindly put me in touch with Simon & Schuster Australia.

▶ CONTENTS ◀

▶ INTRODUCTION ◀

The number of dogs misunderstood by their owners saddens me. In many cases, the owners think they have a very dumb creature on their hands. Yet their dogs look at me with pleading eyes, almost saying, 'Thank God you have arrived. They might be able to understand me now'. This is no reflection on the owners. None of us was born a dog trainer — we all have to learn. I just cannot help feeling sorry for these dogs. I can see their confusion and why, consequently, they act very neurotically. They do something, and then dart for cover. No wonder the owners think their dogs are stupid.

Many dogs surrendered to the RSPCA have behavioural problems. Statements such as 'It's so stupid', 'It's the most destructive dog I have ever had', 'It never shuts up', show that the owner has spent no time on his or her dog's education and yet expects it to behave. I ask these people how *they* would behave if they were never educated or shown how to act in such a way as to fit into society? How would they behave if they were tied up in a backyard, without human contact for hours on end?

Imagine the culture shock for a dog that is naturally a pack animal, born into a litter of pups with a mother that caters to every need, only to have us come along, take it home, put it in our backyard and then leave it all alone when we go to work. It has now become a solitary animal relying on us completely for comfort, companionship and direction. If it does not receive these, then no wonder problems are created.

As a child I had a natural love of animals — especially dogs. Never a week went by that I did not find another one in the street and entice the poor bedraggled thing home with one shilling's worth of devon. They were usually the type of dogs that the owners were glad to see the back of.

They had every problem imaginable. But through trial and error I cured them all.

My grounding as a child and in later years (especially my years at the RSPCA) made me realise the problems untrained dogs can cause. During my 31 years experience, I have discovered that there are a lot of misconceptions about dogs. Despite numerous studies on dog psychology, many people still believe that dogs have human tendencies and think the way we do. This is why many dog owners despair when it comes to their pet's behaviour; they don't understand why their dog doesn't do what they tell it to.

Over the years I have been implored by people who were impressed by my knowledge of dogs and my ability to get them to do almost anything, to write a book on dog training. I have read many such books myself, but felt they were often far too complicated for someone who is just starting out with his or her first dog and needs only a simple explanation and an easy-to-follow cure for behavioural problems, without reams and reams of text. There was a need for a book that explained why a certain problem occurs and how to cure that problem.

My dilemma was how to write a book which explained how a dog's mind worked and how to train it — but still keep the text simple. So simple that anyone could understand it and then be able to cure their dog's behavioural problem. I sincerely hope that this is what I have achieved.

BARK BUSTERS has been written with the express purpose of helping people enjoy owning a dog, since I believe this should be a pleasure and not a problem. This book is about curing your dog of those behavioural problems that mar a potentially perfect relationship between you and your pet. It will show you how to discipline your dog to good behaviour — so that it can enjoy being owned by you, and not have to spend its life being yelled at or tied on a chain or penned up.

I have been to homes where the dog totally ran the house, making its owners' lives miserable. These dogs would either bark frantically or bite to maintain their dominant position in the household hierarchy. This book aims to help you take the control or leadership away from your dog and return it to its rightful place — to you. I will explain why *you* must be the boss and the reason your dog might behave as though *it* is, and you will see why any attempts you have made up to now to make your dog behave properly may not have worked. I will explain when to reprimand and how, when to praise and how, and the way to communicate with your dog.

Life with a trouble-free dog can be a pleasure, and how you can achieve this is detailed in the following pages. So read on!

▶ PART ONE ◀

UNDERSTANDING YOUR DOG AND TEACHING IT THE BASICS

If you wish to train your dog successfully, you must
first understand what its behaviour is based on.
The training techniques given in this book are
based upon this fundamental understanding.

► CHAPTER ONE ◄

Understanding Your Dog

Not being able to understand their dog and how it thinks is where most people fail. They wrongly believe that their dog thinks the same way they do. They say things like 'It knows it's done wrong', 'It understands everything I say'. If your dog really does understand every word you say (and to be realistic, it is highly unlikely) and is still being naughty, then you would have to conclude that your pet is being vindictive and sometimes even masochistic. In cases where dogs show chronic behavioural problems, their owners sometimes take the drastic and completely insupportable measure of physically belting their dog for its misdemeanours. But these dogs still continue their bad habits. Why?

When at their wits' end, such dog owners call me, I ask myself why would a dog suffer punishment and still behave badly, but then stop misbehaving as soon as I trained it without using any harsh treatment? To me, the answer is clear: the owner is not communicating with his or her dog. To communicate successfully with your dog, you must first know what you should be able to expect from it and why it does certain things.

WHAT CAN I EXPECT FROM MY DOG?

Your dog is not a solitary animal. It needs companionship and leadership. In their wild state, dogs live in packs. The most dominant dog (not necessarily male) leads the pack, and the subsequent pecking order depends on the relative dominance of each other member of the group. A dog would not be at the bottom of the pack by choice, but because it does not have the courage, temperament or strength to have a higher standing. Dogs know only pack law: that the strongest, most dominant dog will rule. So if your dog is misbehaving, it is possibly because you are not getting the message of what is correct behaviour through to it or because you have not established dominance over your dog.

Dogs without leadership, especially those that are incapable of it, become confused without a leader. So, if you are the owner of a bottom-of-the-pack type and you are not supplying enough discipline, it will become confused and exhibit unpredictable, erratic behaviour. If, on the other hand, you have a dominant dog and it does not consider you its superior, then you won't be able to control it: your dog won't behave itself if it does not respect you.

WHAT DOES MY DOG EXPECT FROM ME?

A dog needs education. In its natural environment, a dog is educated by the others in its pack. They teach it how to hunt, to play and all the other talents it needs to survive. They also discipline it. Teaching obedience provides us (the dog owners) with a way to establish dominance gradually and take the place of the pack leader.

Many dog owners agonise over their naughty dogs, wishing their pets were capable of even doing the basics: the sit, the stay, and so on. How often have I heard, 'I only want my dog to be well behaved. I don't want it to jump through hoops!' And dog owners are not the only ones who benefit from training: a disobedient or undisciplined dog is like a human without a job; its life has no direction. In every case I have treated, the dog became happier and more contented once it was taught to obey.

During one of my training sessions, the owner, the dog and I were doing some street therapy, teaching the dog how to walk on a lead, when we passed a lady who indignantly said, 'It's a dog, not a robot!' Obviously this lady felt that

TWO BABIES STARTING OUT IN LIFE

Just like a child, your dog needs to be educated. In the wild it would be taught to behave by the pack; in our world, it's our responsibility.

dog training was cruel, and some misinformed people will bombard you with this type of philosophy. But surely it is far kinder to have a dog abide by a few simple rules than to have it causing havoc in our homes or on our streets?

It stands to reason that owning a dog means we have a responsibility to give it an education. We need to teach it the things it needs to know to survive in our society: we need to teach it right from wrong. Dogs do not deliberately do wrong. With little or no proper training, they simply fall into bad habits or they simply do what comes naturally to them. Hundreds of dogs are needlessly destroyed each year because their owners failed to recognise their dogs' needs and did not give them direction. It is our responsibility to ensure that our dogs do not become a nuisance to our neighbours or to society in general. How can we expect dogs to do the right thing if we do not teach them what we expect from them?

HOW DOES MY DOG'S MIND WORK?

In order for your dog to be obedient, it must first of all know that you are the leader, and then it must understand what you want from it. You cannot just expect that your dog will behave well — it must first learn right from wrong. People often ask me, 'Why won't my dog come when it's called?' My answer to this is always the same, 'Have you trained your dog to come to you when it's called?' And their answer to my question is always 'No'. But how can we expect our dog to come to us when we call it, if we have not trained it to do so?

Dogs are very intelligent animals, but they are not mind readers! In the same way we learn things by example, so do dogs. But you cannot show your dog something one day, and then expect it to remember it the next. Like children learning multiplication tables, repetition is needed for the lesson to sink in.

Dogs learn by experience. You can't just explain things to them. Unlike a human being who can be told not to touch a stove because it is hot, to communicate the same thing to a dog, we would physically have to place its paw on the stove. (By the way, I am not for one moment suggesting you do that!) If, however, your dog were to touch the stove accidentally, it would probably never touch it again after experiencing the heat and subsequent pain. Indeed, many dogs develop phobias from just one bad experience. If this happens at the vet's, for example, they will always react badly to going there again.

CASE HISTORY: I remember a boxer dog I was training years ago. Everytime I tried to walk him past a certain paddock, he would start to play up, jumping and dancing around at the end of the lead. After a few days' training, however, I was able to get him to walk calmly past. I later discovered from the dog's owner that the dog had been stung by a bee in that same paddock.

You see, even though the dog had been walked safely past that paddock for months prior to being stung, it only took one bad experience to undo all the good ones.

One way to cure a phobia like the boxer's is to re-establish a good experience by taking a treat with you and giving it to the dog when you get to the location that upsets it. This will only work, however, if the dog is crazy about its food. Another way is to reprimand the dog for silly behaviour and insist it walks past the area properly. (How to reprimand effectively is discussed in the following chapter.) Show the dog that the bad event is not going to happen again, and praise it once it calms down.

I am not suggesting that you use food to train your dog as a rule, since this form of bribery does not establish pack leadership, but I do feel that in certain situations food has its uses. I only use food when I need to distract a dog from what is happening around it. In my opinion, reprimand and praise are the most effective ways to train your dog — and the most hassle-free.

Dogs do not have analytical minds, but mainly rely on experience and instinct. A dog's mind is basically a memory machine. Like a computer it can store things, then on a key word it will respond. A dog learns by association, as shown in the boxer and the bee sting story.

CASE HISTORY: The owners of a silkie terrier had tried unsuccessfully to train it to walk on a lead for almost two years before I was called in.

On my first attempt to cure the dog, I noticed its absolute fear of the lead; it would not budge when the lead was on. I tried food, coaxing and all my usual techniques, but the dog was not interested. When I asked the owner if the dog had had a bad experience on the lead, she replied 'Definitely not. We have never been able to get her on a lead to take her anywhere!' Though this was puzzling, it really did not matter what made the terrier behave the way she did, the cure was training. I finally discovered that if I got down on all fours with the lead in my hand and as long as I did not face her, the silkie would take a few steps. I just repeated 'Come on' over and over again to teach her the command. Two hours later I was making good progress.

I returned the next day to complete the training, and the owner told me she had worked out what had disturbed the dog. It seems that the owner had had to go into hospital when the dog was only young, leaving her two sons to care for the pup. While in hospital, she asked the boys to take the pup to the groomers. Can you imagine how scary a grooming parlour would be to a young pup? All those strangers and all those dogs! So from then on, the dog associated the lead with that upsetting experience and every time its owners put the lead on their pet, it freaked out.

In training the silkie I was able to show it that the bad experience it had once received on the lead would not necessarily happen again, and it now happily goes for walks with its owners.

HOW A DOG'S PACK MENTALITY AND ITS LEARNING BY EXPERIENCE MAY COMBINE …

What we think of as a bad experience — and one we don't want to be repeated — may be perceived differently by a dog. My dog, Laddie, chased cars and was run over many times as a result, but he only seemed to become more aggressive towards cars after each experience. Yet when I (in my role as leader) reprimanded Laddie for chasing cars, he ceased his bad behaviour out of respect for me. In the same way, an aggressive dog would soon stop misbehaving if the pack leader were to make it known that it was not at all pleased.

(Laddie was afraid of water, so I was able to cure his bad habit by throwing plastic bags filled with water at him whenever he chased cars.)

The thing that encourages a dog to chase cars is the sense of victory achieved when, after having barked at and chased an approaching car, it 'runs away'. Should the car run the dog over, a dominant dog will attack again because, from the dog's perspective, the car has no authority to reprimand it. Overcoming a dog's natural tendencies which can lead to bad behaviour, requires persistence.

DOG TEMPERAMENTS

Understanding your dog's temperament will help you to train it and thus help it understand what you want from it.

What Will My Dog Be Like to Train?

I have discovered that the temperament of a dog has nothing to do with its size, environment, upbringing, treatment or breed. I remember a dog that was surrendered to the RSPCA after five years of abuse by its owner. Yet I would have defied anyone to pick the dog out from all the other dogs in the kennels — it was a very happy animal. Another two dogs had spent twelve months locked in a small box, receiving only nourishment but no love or care. Other than a little depression, they showed no signs of timidness.

I believe a dog's temperament is something it is born with. Good basic training will improve certain traits, of course, but you can never change a dog's basic temperament. I have observed hundreds of puppies over the years, and I can always spot the nervous, the timid, the dominant, and the middle-of-the-pack types, even from an early age, in every litter.

Good breeding does play a big part in eliminating the undesirable types. Many breeders are now seriously looking at temperament. No breeder worth their salt would breed an undesirable temperament in favour of a dog's good looks.

The nervous, timid little fellow that wets the floor each time you scold it is an example of an undesirable temperament. That is not to say that it cannot be trained or that it does not deserve your love, but the results from training will not be as successful as those in a dog that is not nervous. I have successfully cured hundreds of nervous dogs of their annoying behavioural problems. The dogs are quite often still left with other less annoying problems but their owners are invariably prepared to live with them because, despite everything, they still love their dogs very much and understand that what they have achieved is the best they can expect in view of the dog's temperament.

There are four basic temperament types dogs can have: *Timid* temperaments will respond quickly to training, while *nervous* types need more persistence; these are bottom-of-the-pack dogs. *Dominant* (strong-willed) temperaments need consistency, dominance and a prolonged all-out effort on the part of the trainer to succeed; these are top-of-the-pack dogs. Then we come to those with a middle-of-the-road temperament, which I call *middle-of-the-pack*. This type is neither timid nor nervous and is not strong-willed. It trains quickly because it wants to please. It is undoubtedly the best temperament of all.

What Type of Temperament Does My Dog Have?

So, how can you pick what type of temperament your dog has? This is where the fun begins.

A *timid* dog might appear quite naughty and disobedient, so you might think it's not timid at all. But a timid dog can behave this way if it sees you as further down the pack than itself; in other words, if you are not displaying

Timid dogs are generally easy to identify: they tend to hold back their ears, tuck their tails between their legs and squirm or roll on their backs.

dominant tendencies. You see, if you put two very submissive dogs together, one will still become the pack leader, but if you introduce a more dominant dog to the scenario, it will quickly establish itself as leader. In all cases, the dominant dog will rule the pack.

To determine the type of temperament your dog has, you will need to watch the way the dog behaves around your family, visitors and friends. Watch your dog closely when it meets strangers or people outside the household. A timid dog will hold its ears back, squirm about, put its tail between its legs or roll on its back. If your dog displays these tendencies with strangers but is totally different with you or your family, then you have the timid type, which will train easily once it knows you are the leader.

Most people can recognise a *nervous* dog, but again there is a sliding scale — your dog might be quite at home with you, but very nervous of strangers. A nervous dog will normally bark at a stranger, then back off the instant the stranger enters the property. These nervous types can

Nervous dogs may behave quite happily with you but become disturbed by the presence of strangers. They will frequently bark or growl and may either hide or circle the stranger and even try to attack from behind.

behave in several different ways: they might run off as soon as a stranger enters your property, and either hide under the lounge or circle the area barking and growling; some will run aggressively and try to attack from behind; others will settle down once the stranger is seated, but will start barking the moment the visitor rises to leave and may even try to attack. This type of dog is difficult to train because quite often the fear of the stranger will overcome the fear of a reprimand.

A dog with a *dominant* (strong-willed) temperament is very hard to control. When strangers arrive this dog is likely to put its tail high in the air, stand its ground and will, under certain circumstances, attack. You will need to be consistent and assertive with this dog. If you move too quickly it could bite you; it will not relinquish its leadership easily, and you might even need expert assistance. Do try training the dog yourself first — it all boils down to dominance. With regular programming and consistency

Dominant dogs will stand as tall as they can, hold their tails and ears erect and will walk with stiff legs. They will stand their ground in the presence of strangers and may even attack.

Dogs that have a middle-of-the-pack temperament are well-balanced and are generally confident around strangers and do not, as a rule, show aggression towards other dogs.

from you, even the strongest willed dog can be controlled. Be determined: it will pay dividends in the end.

If your dog does not fit into any of these categories then it has the temperament of a dog from the *middle of the pack*. This dog is usually friendly to strangers, confident and not usually aggressive to other dogs. Once programmed, this type will train easily and once it is cured of any bad habits, will be a delight to own. It is usually a well-adjusted dog that loves everybody.

How Should I Deal with My Dog's Temperament?

How well you deal with your dog's particular temperament will, of course, depend on your own temperament. Just as dogs have a set personality, so do we. My daughter recently asked me to pick out a puppy for her from a litter. I knew that it would need to be a dog from the top of the pack, without any nervousness, as a timid dog would drive her to distraction because of her assertive personality. She needed a dog that would train easily, once dominated, and one that would be frightened of nothing. On the other hand, my son would be more at home with a dog from the middle of the pack, as its temperament type would suit his personality, rather than a dominant dog which would conflict with him every day. Just how you should respond to your dog's particular temperament, and how tough you will need to be to gain control, is detailed below.

Timid Type
This dog won't need you to be too dominant to control it. Be consistent; do not allow it to get away with something today because you feel sorry for it, then reprimand it tomorrow because you have lost your temper. Train this dog on a daily basis, as it is the best way to gain the upper hand over this type of temperament. It won't need a lot of aggression from you, just a set training routine.

Nervous Type
Nervy dogs are always difficult to deal with, even for experienced trainers. I have found the most effective way

to approach this type is to be very tough, otherwise their nerves will take over and you will lose control. Do not pity this dog; stand firm, or all your efforts will get you nowhere. Your results will never be perfect but you can certainly greatly improve things. I remember a Yorkshire terrier I once found at a dog pound. I was looking for a small dog to train for the stage musical *Gypsy*. The dog I found was tiny, nervy and could not sit still for a minute. It was also very snappy and possessive. Yet with the correct training (which included carrying the dog a lot to reassure and accustom it to handling), this little dog took part in fourteen performances without any hitches. So be firm, do not relent and you will get satisfactory results.

Dominant Type
Dominant dogs are not for the timid; a dog like this will not be controlled by a less-dominant personality. You will need to earn this dog's respect. It has nothing to do with size, and everything to do with consistency and dominant behaviour. A dominant person would not walk away from a dog that growled at them. They would retaliate.

CASE HISTORY: One of my first dogs was a German shepherd named Monty, whose temperament made him top of the pack. With proper handling and training he went on to become an Australian Obedience Champion. One day, however, when he was about ten years old, I went towards Monty to pick up the bone he was happily chewing so I could move him to his kennel, and he growled at me for the first time. I could not believe my ears. Monty had been bone trained from a very early age and had to this day given no resistance to myself or my children touching his food. I knew I had to retaliate, otherwise he would think me a pushover. I grabbed his check chain and shook him, then went to take the bone again. Again he growled at me. This continued for about ten minutes until he relented. I instinctively knew I could not walk away from this. He never growled at me or any member of my family again.

I later discovered that the reason for his over-protectiveness of his food was because my son and daughter, who were only six and seven at the time, had been taking Monty's bones away from him and giving them to our female German shepherd, Sheba, because she was pregnant. Even armed with that information, I knew I still had done the right thing.

Dominance and consistency are essential to gain control over the pack-leader type. If the task proves too daunting, seek professional assistance.

Middle-of-the-pack Type

This type is usually a delight to own once they are trained and cured of any problems. You will still need to display dominant, consistent behaviour, and this dog will need to know that you still have what it takes to be the leader. Insisting on obedience is the best way to convince a dog that you are in control.

I truly believe all dogs are beautiful and, in the right hands, any type of temperament can be trained.

POPULAR MISCONCEPTIONS

As mentioned at the beginning of this book, there are many misconceptions where dogs are concerned. I guess the reason for this is because we cannot sit the dog down and ask it how it thinks, what it sees, or how it feels. The list of misconceptions is long and varied:

You cannot teach an old dog new tricks. Of course you can. Dogs are no different from us. One old dog I trained had never been on a lead in its fourteen years and was lead trained successfully in one two-hour session.

It was mistreated as a pup, that is why it is the way it is. Not true. A dog's temperament is something it is born with. But, whatever a dog's temperament, it can be trained to behave well.

It will grow out of it. Not always true. Puppies may chew things when they are teething, or they may dig for the pleasure of activity. Dogs can grow out of these behaviours, but not always. If bad habits continue, a dog needs to be trained out of them.

He's a sled dog and therefore a natural puller. All dogs are natural pullers; a man in Alaska has a sled team of standard poodles. However, this does not mean a dog has no choice but to pull you madly down the street. All dogs can be trained to walk properly on a lead.

When we leave our dog it wrecks the garden out of spite. A dog does get upset when you leave it, but it wrecks the garden more out of stress than spite.

It understands every word I say. No it does not. Tie a dog up in a park somewhere and then tell it you will be back in a minute. It will get upset and when it barks, I doubt very much that *you* will understand a word it is saying. How often have you seen a dog turn its head from side to side when someone is talking to it? It's because dogs do not have a clue what we are saying. We need to teach them our language.

When my dog jumps on me, it's doing it because it loves me. Not true. Your dog is going for height to be more dominant, or because of bad habits it learnt as a pup.

If I treat my dog with love and kindness, it will, in turn, treat me with love and kindness. Not true. I have met hundreds of people who treat their dogs like kings and queens and the dogs in turn bite and attack them. Not all dogs are like this, I know, but it is what can happen if a dog only has love in its life and no discipline.

Dogs should be allowed to bark because it's their only way of expressing themselves. It is true that dogs enjoy barking, but then again children enjoy screaming. Just as we can expect that our children should not run through the house screaming, we can expect that our dog can also obey some rules.

Obedience training is cruel. If that is the case, then sending our children to school is cruel. We must be responsible for our dog's well-being if we wish to keep a dog in our society — and that includes educating it. If we do not take responsibility for our dogs, the day will dawn when responsible dog owners will be made to pay for those who are irresponsible. The signs are already appearing with councils issuing heavy fines for strays and noisy dogs. There are now so many rules governing dog ownership and so many places where they are unwelcome that dogs and dog lovers will be the losers in the end.

It is cruel to keep a dog cooped up in the backyard all the time. It certainly isn't ideal to keep a dog cooped up in a backyard *all* the time, but sometimes it is the only option owners have. Dogs do not have a conscience; they can just as easily chase and kill a goat or chicken as attack a child. It may be that the only way you can keep your dog out of trouble is by enclosing it in the backyard when you aren't around and then supervising it when other people, especially children, are present. In any case, a dog should never be free to roam the streets at will.

Once you allow a dog freedom, it's very hard to take it back. It's much easier to confine the dog in the first place and then to take it out for supervised walks regularly. If you do keep a dog in the backyard, make sure you give it plenty of exercise and, as always, companionship.

CASE HISTORY: I remember two Great Danes who had to be put to sleep because they had turned into goat and sheep killers. Their owner had allowed them to roam while he was at work and they had taken to chasing stock at a nearby farm on a daily basis. The farmer didn't know who they belonged to and, as they were only chasing for fun, did not, at first, think it would present a great problem. When their owner arrived home, the dogs were always there to greet him. He had no idea that anything was wrong. His feelings were, he told me later, that two huge dogs needed room to roam. He realises now they needed supervised walks. Eventually the farmer found out where the dogs lived, and informed their owner that they had spooked one of his valuable racehorses, which had fallen and broken its leg and had to be destroyed. After that,

the owner did attempt to keep the dogs confined to their
backyard but because of the freedom they had previously enjoyed,
the dogs escaped by jumping the fence and so their owner was
unable to keep them in. When the owner discovered that his dogs
had started to attack sheep and goats, he had the dogs put down.

Penning a dog is cruel. Penning a dog is not the most
desirable solution to a problem, but some people have no
choice, especially if their yard doesn't have a fence. When
confining a dog, be sure the dog is well-protected and has
ample room to stretch its legs. Penning is far preferable
to chaining a dog. Providing the dog receives lots of
exercise, penning is quite acceptable.

Desexing a dog makes it fat. Not true. Desexing a dog will
probably increase its interest in food, but food is what
makes the dog fat. Desexing is beneficial to stop unwanted
pregnancies in female dogs and likewise in the male dog
to stop it mating.

Desexing a dog, especially a male dog, is cruel. Desexing
a dog is not cruel. If anything, it's far kinder, especially
if you do not intend to breed the dog. If a male is desexed
it will no longer be worried if it lives next to a bitch in
season. In many cases, desexing will prevent fence-jumping
for this reason. It also reduces aggression: mainly in male
dogs, towards other male dogs. Therefore desexing a dog
at an early age it will help keep it from fighting. Desexing
is not the entire answer to a dog being well-behaved but
it is a step in the right direction.

A dog can become vicious once it has tasted blood. If that
is the case then you would not be able to feed a dog raw
meat. If your dog kills a rabbit or chicken, it does not
necessarily mean that it will attack you or your children.
It is quite natural for a dog to stalk and kill prey — that
is how it survived in the wild. It did not then return to
the pack and attack and kill one of the other members.

I suspect the saying 'You won't stop him now he's tasted
blood' comes from the fact that once a dog has got into

the habit of killing chickens or stock, it will keep on killing unless trained to stop. It is no different from a dog that develops a habit of chasing cars. If a dog does become vicious, it's most probably because of bad training, not because it has tasted blood.

KEY POINTS

- There are many misconceptions about dogs. Understanding your dog is the key to knowing what to expect from it and how to train it.

- Your dog does not understand every word you say. Nor does it have an analytical, rational mind.

- Only through experience will your dog learn what you want from it.

- Dogs need leadership. Your dog will do what you want only if it sees you as more dominant than itself and therefore to be respected.

- Your dog needs education. When you discipline your dog, you are giving it the incentive to do the right thing.

- Whatever the temperament of your dog, with the right approach, problems can be overcome and your dog successfully trained.

▶ CHAPTER TWO ◀

Educating Your Dog

The most important tool in training your dog is your voice — the words you say and how you say them. Next comes your body language and the signs and signals you use. Before any training can begin, it is vital that you understand how to communicate with your dog. The actual equipment you use in training your dog is, of course, very important and is also discussed in this chapter.

ESTABLISHING COMMUNICATION

Just as *we* had to learn our language as babies, dogs have to be trained to understand our commands. People often complain that their dogs won't do what they are told, but, as I always ask, have the animals been *trained* to know what their owners mean when they give a command? Dogs don't speak English! Do *you* understand what your dog means when it barks?

The best way to understand your dog and its language is to look at the way it relates to other dogs. Dogs do not have a language like ours: their language consists of a combination of gutteral sounds, such as growling and barking, and body language. From a very early age, a puppy learns that if it does not respond to a growl from another member of the pack, it will be followed by a nip or some other form of discipline. The pup soon understands that a growl is a warning that will be followed by something far worse. If the pup wants to avoid the physical discipline, it learns to stop whatever it is doing at the sound of the growl. It is a very simple communication of cause and effect. So, if a dog wants to reprimand another dog, it will growl. It will not say 'Shut up you mongrel dog'.

In view of a dog's simple language, it stands to reason that in order for you to teach your pet *your* language, you must keep it simple. Use basic, simple words like 'sit', 'good boy' and 'stay'. Sentences such as 'Just you sit here while I go over there: don't follow me', are far too complicated for the dog.

I've discovered the most effective word to train a dog is 'Bah' because it is the nearest we can get to a growl. The word 'No' (which is widely used by many trainers) just doesn't come close. Try using both words in turn, in a very harsh tone. You will notice 'Bah' is far more effective than 'No'. Programming means educating your dog to the meaning of the word 'Bah'. It involves letting the dog know that if it does not respond to this reprimand, consequences will follow. How to programme your dog is discussed later in this chapter (see page 32).

Voice Tones

The tone of your voice is very important to your dog because this is what it primarily recognises. Your dog will, in time, come to recognise a word if it is used often enough, but voice tones are especially important in the early stages of training and reprimanding your pet.

There are three different tones of voice you should use when training your dog. These are:

Normal speaking voice: To be used for your commands such as 'sit', 'drop', 'stay', etc.

Harsh growling voice: To be used when saying 'Bah' to reprimand your dog.

Soft melodic voice: To be used for praise, such as 'He's a good boy!'

Body Language

Body language plays a big part in a dog's communication with other dogs. A dominant dog will draw itself up as tall as it can, its tail and ears erect, and will walk with stiff legs when approaching another dog. A timid dog will crouch as low as possible, letting the other dog know it is no threat. It will sometimes even roll over, exposing its belly. (This is why, when training the recall (see page 34), I recommend crouching because by using the posture of submission, you encourage the dog to come to you.)

'Freezing the action' is a posture that I mention in a lot of the cures for bad behaviour (for example, in 'Jumping Up', page 64). It resembles a dominant dog's body language when it walks very stiffly, keeping its body movements to a minimum. Freezing the action of your body helps control the over-activity of a very exuberant dog that may be misbehaving by jumping at you or playfully biting you. By freezing the action and growling 'Bah', you are emulating the way a dominant dog would reprimand another dog, and it is something the dog can instinctively relate to.

In summing up, the best way to communicate with your dog is by using the vocal and body language it can understand.

The Most Important Language of All: Praise

Although much of this book is taken up with the ways and means of reprimanding your dog, these techniques are used only to achieve one thing: to let your dog know what you want from it. They are not meant as forms of punishment for bad behaviour, but rather as a direct language of communication with your dog. None of the techniques in this book should be performed in anger at a dog's misbehaviour; they are controlled training methods.

In every case of training, the most important reinforcement for good behaviour is praise. You can yell at your dog a hundred times for doing something wrong, but, as already explained, this won't mean that it will understand *what* you're angry about. Knowing *how* to reprimand correctly will give you the opportunity to praise your dog.

Whenever your dog does something you've asked it to or stops its bad behaviour, let it know you are pleased with it. Praise your dog in a soft, melodic voice, using the same words every time, such as 'Good boy', 'Good girl'. It is important that your dog understands that these are words of praise because it may not always be possible for you to pat the dog when it does the right thing (for example, if it's some distance from you). Of course, when your dog is near, pat it warmly.

PREPARING YOURSELF: WHAT EQUIPMENT DO I NEED?

The equipment you use to train your dog is important. Many people I visit during private home tuition have equipment inadequate for their training needs. Such things as chain leads (which make it impossible to hold a difficult dog) and ordinary leather collars serve no purpose when it comes to training or walking your dog. Below is a list of the essential equipment you will need. The items marked with an asterisk are optional, as they will only be necessary to cure your dog if it has problems which require these items. (See the chapters in Part 2 of this book which are related to solving specific problems in your dog.)

Essential Equipment

- 2 metre (6 foot) soft webbing lead
- Check chain (10 centimetres [4 inches] longer than the dog's neck size and with a thick gauge)
- Throw chain (available from hardware stores, buy 3 metres [10 feet] of utility chain and have it cut into four pieces)
- Plastic sandwich bags*
- Wok or steel colander*

Equipment you will need to train your dog:
1. Long, soft webbing lead; 2. Check chain; 3. Throw chain; 4. Plastic sandwich bags; 5. Wok or metal colander; 6. Lightweight, long lead; 7. Drink can half-filled with pebbles; 8. Water sprayer; 9. Bucket.

- 5 metre (16 foot) lightweight long lead (made with mower cord, snap lock and leather handle)
- Empty drink can (half-filled with pebbles)*
- Water sprayer*
- Bucket*

*As mentioned in the previous paragraph, the items marked with an asterisk are optional.

How to Use a Throw Chain

The purpose of a throw chain is to reinforce your reprimand, not your command. In other words, if you want to stop your dog from biting your hands, for example, and your reprimand word fails to stop it, then toss your throw chain near the dog's feet. But you should never throw the chain at your dog if it fails to respond to a command such as 'Sit'. The 'Bah' word combined with checking the lead should be the only reprimands you use in that situation.

The throw chain also helps you gain control when the dog is off-lead — it replaces the check chain and lead. Your dog reacts to the sound it makes, the same way it reacts to the sound of the check chain. Whenever your dog misbehaves, throw the chain as if you are trying to hit the dog but deliberately miss; try to get as close as possible to the animal. The throw chain is not designed to hit the dog, but if you do connect by accident, it will not hurt it since all the edges of the chain are rounded.

It may be necessary to throw the chain several times for some dogs to catch on. As soon as the dog responds to the use of the throw chain, praise it. If your dog runs away and hides, call it to you and praise it lavishly. Your dog must be rewarded when it does the right thing. Keep your commands as simple as possible. You will only need two verbal commands: 'Bah' when the dog does the wrong thing; and 'Good boy' or 'Good girl' as praise for the instant it behaves properly.

The most important training aids are immediate action, the throw chain, the voice reprimand 'Bah', and consistency.

If your dog becomes aggressive when you try to pick up the chain, then tie a piece of lightweight rope to your chain, so that you can pick it up without bending down (which puts you in a vulnerable position), or keep several throw chains. It's important to be persistent with this dog — you need to overcome its aggression.

If the dog's behaviour doesn't improve, you may need to put the dog on-lead so that you can stay in control of the situation. The instant the dog becomes aggressive, lift its paws off the ground for a few seconds and shake it. (Shaking the dog is similar to how a pack leader would reprimand another dog.) Of course, always keep your own safety in mind and if you find your dog too difficult to handle, seek professional help.

How to Use the Check Chain

Check chains are the most maligned pieces of training equipment, mainly because very few instructions come with them. Numbers of people call it a 'choker chain' and wrongly think that it is designed to be used as punishment. Many people give up on check chains, branding them cruel and useless, but, if used correctly, the check chain is the kindest way to walk and train your dog.

Your dog is only meant to react to the metallic sound the chain makes each time it is snapped back and immediately released. It's not designed to be pulled taut all the time. If used correctly, the chain is *never* pulled completely tight. If your dog over-reacts to the check chain, it will only be reacting to the sound, rather than any pain the chain inflicts.

If, when you put the check chain on, your dog does react badly, squealing, jumping around, and so on, leave it on,

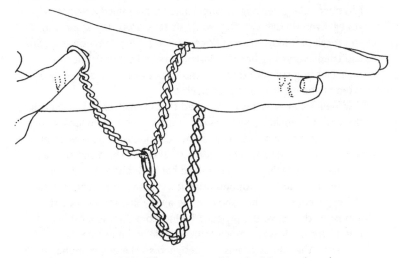

The check chain should be 10 centimetres (4 inches) longer than the circumference of your dog's neck and should be made from a thick gauged chain. It should be fitted so that the connecting link falls to the dog's right side.

under supervision, for five to ten minutes a day until the dog has accepted the chain happily. It is not wise to leave a check chain on a dog unless you are in attendance. Many dogs have come to grief while left alone wearing a check chain: the chain becomes caught on a fence or gets wrapped around a pole and the dog chokes itself through trying to pull away.

Ideally the check chain should be no longer than 10 centimetres (4 inches) larger than the dog's neck size. Simply measure the dog's neck and add 10 centimetres to calculate the size of the check chain you should buy.

There is a right and a wrong way to place the check chain on the dog. With the dog on your left side, place the chain on its neck. The chain should check and release easily. If it snags, take it off and turn it around. Another way to ensure it's on the right way is to hold it in the shape of a 'P' when facing the dog.

CASE HISTORY: The owner of a two-year-old Jack Russell terrier had been taking her dog to obedience training since it was very young. Even though the dog would sit stay, drop stay, stand stay and recall perfectly, the owner could not get it to heel on-lead. She had tried everything her club instructors had advised, but to no avail. Her dog still pulled to the end of the lead and refused every attempt she made to get it to heel.

When I took over I was intrigued that even after all the training the dog still wouldn't heel. I asked the owner if I could look at her equipment. She showed me a leather check chain and a webbing lead. I asked if she had ever tried a steel check chain and she said she had: the training club had issued her with one when she first started, but she had stopped using it because it was cutting into the dog's neck. She then showed me a very fine steel check chain, almost as thin as wire. I produced mine from my bag to show her the difference; it was a much thicker chain and much heavier. I explained that check chains are designed so the dog responds to the noise it makes, not to any choking. I rattled both chains in turn, showing the lady the noise mine made compared to hers, which hardly made any sound at all. Due to the fineness of the gauge, all her chain could actually do was hurt the dog. I was shocked that even a renowned dog club did not fully understand the way a check chain works.

With the correct equipment, I trained the dog to walk properly at heel in half an hour.

Be sure to select a reasonably sized gauge and steer clear of very fine chains which will only hurt your dog's neck.

The Training Lead

The length of your training lead should be at least 2 metres (6 feet) long. Shorter leads are nearly impossible to hold correctly and still give enough slack to the dog. A strong, difficult dog is a lot harder to control on a short lead because it gives the dog too much leverage.

Equipment You Should Not Use

- Rolled-up newspaper
- Chain leads
- Extra long or very fine check chains
- Short leads (less than 2 metres [6 feet] long)

Why You Shouldn't Use a Rolled-Up Newspaper

An old method of disciplining a dog, which is still in use, is the rolled-up newspaper. I am strongly opposed to this method of discipline. I have heard many experts claim that it doesn't hurt the dog. Well, you roll up a newspaper and try hitting yourself with it! Or better still, have someone else hit you with it. And this is the method people are advised to use on their puppy! The experts' claim is silly anyway: if it does not hurt, then what earthly use is it? What incentive would a fully grown Rottweiler have for fearing it? None. In my experience it only makes a dog more aggressive towards its owner — or more frustrated.

The glaring fault in this type of reprimand is that you are not letting your dog know why you are displeased with

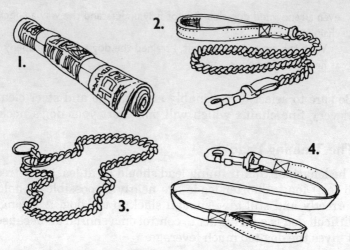

Equipment that should never be used to train your dog:
1. Rolled newspaper; 2. Chain lead; 3. Fine gauged or very long check chains; 4. Short leads.

it. Say, for example, the dog is in the yard barking at the back door. The scenario goes something like this: you hear the dog barking, so you pick up the paper, go to the back door, open it and belt the dog. Naturally enough it cowers away and you go back inside and close the door. A couple of minutes go by, and the dog starts to bark again. So once more, you pick up the newspaper, and ...

Now let's look at it from the dog's point of view. It's outside and wants to come in to be with you but the door bars its way. So the dog barks to remind you it is there. The door opens, and wham! Then the door shuts and the dog is *still* outside but with a sore nose. Of course it will bark again. You see, the reason the dog is not catching on is that by the time it receives the reprimand for barking at the back door, the back door is open and you are there (just what it wanted), but then bang! you hit the dog. The reprimand does not happen at the precise moment it was barking. It happens seconds later. Too late for your poor pet to connect the reprimand with the action that led to the reprimand.

What should have happened is this: the dog is barking at the back door, so you sneak to an open window near the dog and while it continues to bark you throw an object which will make a lot of noise (such as a drink can half-filled with pebbles) as close to it as possible, and yell 'Bah'. This will startle it. It makes more sense — the dog receives the reprimand at the precise moment that it is doing the wrong thing. It is much more effective than a confusing clout with a newspaper.

Why You Shouldn't Use Chain Leads

Chain leads look very attractive but they serve no purpose when it comes to training a dog; a soft webbing lead is far gentler on your hands when trying to control a dog that is pulling. To train a dog, you need to be able to hold on to all of the lead at some time or other, and the chain lead will not give your hands a comfortable grip.

SUCCESSFUL PROGRAMMING

Programming means teaching your dog what *not* to do by training it to respond to a particular form of reprimand. Training itself generally refers to the methods involved in teaching your dog how to do things (the sit, the stay, etc.). Hence, even dogs that have been trained need to be programmed to the 'Bah' reprimand and the throw chain if their behavioural problems are to be cured.

Although your dog's initial programming will take place in the backyard, to cure specific behavioural problems, it makes sense that a dog should be programmed in the particular location in which it misbehaves. For example, if your dog misbehaves in the house, it should be programmed in the house. It is unreasonable to expect that your dog will be able to connect what it has learned with knowing that it's not allowed to jump up on you, for example, when you walk out the back door. (If this is the case, programming in this specific situation will also need to take place in the backyard.)

To discipline or reprimand your dog successfully, you will need to discover how forceful you have to be in order to get it to respond. The best way to do this is to start simply, using just a stern voice reprimand ('Bah!') in conjunction with a throw chain or a drink can half-filled with pebbles. Always reprimand your dog at the very moment it is misbehaving. As I have already explained, dogs cannot make the connection between a reprimand and bad behaviour that they are no longer doing — even if it was just seconds ago.

In extreme cases, with some very determined dogs, you will need to use more physical measures. If your dog fits into this category, make sure you are in control. Always attach a lead to a dog that you suspect will offer you resistance; the lead will give you the upper hand. If you find it impossible to control your dog with the methods I have mentioned so far, you might have to use the lead to lift the dog's front paws off the ground for a couple of seconds, saying 'Bah'. With a very large dog you may need a little extra strength to do this. It should only take seconds. Don't lose your temper — you won't gain anything by being angry. Your dog will not relinquish its leadership easily or without some resistance, so you should always stay in control.

How to Programme Your Dog

Programming takes place in a controlled situation. If your dog is untrained, then teaching your dog to respond to the reprimand will occur while you are obedience training your dog to sit or drop and stay. In this case, refer to the methods outlined in 'Obedience: The Basics', page 34, to make sure you also train your dog correctly. Page references to the relevant sections are given where appropriate.

If your dog is already trained but misbehaves in certain situations, you will still need to follow the stages given in the following pages. If your dog is generally obedient during the sit, the drop and the stay, you will find introducing distractions (Stage 2) very effective in making the dog misbehave and thus enabling you to reprimand it.

Stage 1

Programming should be done on the lead and, initially, in your backyard. Your lead should always be kept slack, as all exercises are working towards eventually having the dog off the lead. Your pet should never be able to feel the lead other than when you check it.

Using your check chain and lead, put your dog in a sit (see page 41) and then command it to stay (see page 44). If it moves from the spot, reprimand it by saying 'Bah' and sit it back down again. It is permissible for your dog to move its head but not its body. The timing of the reprimand is crucial. If your dog gets up and walks over to you, and *then* you say 'Bah', the dog will not understand why it is being reprimanded. Remember, the reprimand must happen at the precise moment your dog makes a mistake in order for it to catch on. Keep practising the sit and reprimand until your dog does it correctly, then praise.

Stage 2

Your dog should be conditioned to obeying you, no matter who is around or what distractions there are. One way of achieving this is to introduce distractions during the programming. Use the 'Bah' reprimand whenever your dog moves from its position.

Distractions should be introduced in stages. First of all, do some crouching. Crouch down in front of your dog while it is in a stay, then try bouncing a ball or placing food on the ground. Next, ask a friend to walk into the yard or walk a dog near the fence, while you have your dog in a stay. Ask children to run around the yard. Run around yourself, bouncing a ball, and so on. All of these things will help to make your dog steady in a stay.

Stage 3

This next step in programming should be commenced once your dog has mastered Stage two. With your dog on its lead, walk towards your side gate. Check your dog with a whiplash type action if it attempts to follow you through the gate, and say 'Bah'. Keep persisting until your dog stops when you approach the gate. Make your dog sit, and then step through the gate yourself. Once your dog is steady, say 'Free', tugging the lead at the same time. Eventually the word on its own will be sufficient. (Use the 'free' command every time you have your dog on a lead, or under your control, and you wish to let it go free.) Praise your dog lavishly when it comes to you. Always make your dog sit and wait for the 'free' command every time you open the gate. This will promote good on and off the lead habits. Remember always to hold your lead slack.

As you can see, the throw chain was not used in any of the above programming. The only time the throw chain should be used is when the dog is off-lead, or in those specific situations (outlined in Part 2 of this book) when it is necessary to keep control over your dog. *Never* throw a chain near a dog for moving from the 'Stay'.

Programming your dog to the throw chain (used in conjunction with the 'Bah' reprimand) can be done during your specific problem-solving training. How to use the throw chain correctly is discussed on page 25.

OBEDIENCE: THE BASICS

Basic obedience is all that most people want from their dog. All that the average person needs or expects is for their dog to come when it is called, to stay when it is told and to be well behaved generally. Simple obedience can be taught quite easily with patience and consistent use of the reprimand word 'Bah' and other reprimand tools.

The Recall

This is the most important thing you can train your dog to do. A dog that won't come when called is an embarrassment, and unless you can get your dog to come to you, there is not much else you can do with it. You will be afraid to let it off the lead because it won't respond to any command, and if it does escape, a wild chase will ensue.

Luckily, it is fairly easy to train a dog to come when called. Your tone of voice is very important here.

CASE HISTORY: The owners of a German shepherd called me in because their dog refused to come when called. As soon as they opened the front door to greet me, a large dog came from behind them, squeezed past their legs, jumped over the front fence and raced across the road and into a large park. Its owners immediately gave chase, yelling at it to come back. The dog took a quick look over its shoulder, saw that its owners were following and then continued bounding away. When I called to them to stop, they said, 'If we don't catch him, he'll be gone for hours'. I asked his name and then knelt down and, in a soft sing-song tone, called 'Here, Shane, come on, good boy', patting my thighs at the same time. The dog spun around and came charging towards me. He nearly knocked me over. Needless to say, his owners were amazed.

Why had the dog come to me — a complete stranger — but refused to respond in any way to his owners? The reason was simple: it was the way they were going about it. First, they were using his name alone; a dog's name should only be used to attract its attention. Just like us, how can a dog be expected to understand what we want from it by just calling its name?

Secondly, you should never chase a dog that refuses to come to you. It will only think the whole performance is a big game or that you are romping with it. If you kneel, crouch or even lie down, the dog will be more likely to come to you. Using a submissive pose like this will encourage the dog to investigate you.

Thirdly, your voice tone is very important. Never use a harsh tone when calling your dog. Never shout or scream and point at your feet. This will only make your dog scared of you because your manner is threatening. (Your dog must never fear coming to you; only fear *not* coming to you.) Never make a grab at your dog's collar; the first thing you should do when the dog approaches you is pat it lavishly. And never allow a dog off the lead if it won't come when called.

To teach your dog to recall, use a 5 metre (16 foot) lightweight lead. Allow your dog to wander with no restrictions to the end of the lead, then call it, tugging on the lead, while crouching down and patting your legs in an inviting way. As soon as your dog comes, praise it lavishly. Never force your dog to come; repeat the exercise several times until it comes happily to you every time.

Fido, come!

Good boy!

You should start your dog's recall training on a 5 metre (16 foot) lightweight training lead. This can be made easily from a mower cord, which can be purchased from your local hardware store and attached to a snap lock. Add an old leather strap or handbag handle to the other end as a handgrip to complete your lead.

Take your dog to a park or paddock, place it on the long lead and either let it be distracted or ask someone to distract it on purpose for a couple of minutes. Then call your dog in this fashion; 'Fido, come', making sure that your voice is inviting. Tug the lead, crouch down, pat your legs and, as soon as the dog reaches you pat it and praise it ('Good boy', 'He's a good boy', etc.). Pat your dog into a sit, putting a small amount of pressure on the hindquarters. Do not force it. Wait for a few seconds and then say 'Free' and call your dog. It must come under its own steam, and not be reeled in like a fish. If your dog proves difficult and refuses to come on the first tug of the lead, then continue tugging, saying 'Bah' during each refusal. You will need to carry out this training on a regular basis for approximately three weeks.

To test your dog off the lead for the first time after training, take it to an enclosed park or yard (not your own). Call the dog in the same manner as during training, saying 'Bah' and throwing your throw chain near its feet if it refuses to come. As soon as it responds, crouch down and praise it. Repeat this method until your dog comes of its own free will.

Super-Quick Method for Recall

This training must be conducted in a fenced field, park or sports ground, and not your backyard. Make sure there is no way the dog can escape. Let your dog off the lead, leaving the check chain on. Allow a minute or so for the dog to investigate its surroundings, then call it to you. Crouch and praise your dog in a soft voice. If it ignores you, throw your throw chain near its back legs and say 'Bah' very harshly. Repeat this until your dog responds, remembering always to change your tone the instant the dog looks at you or shows some sign of coming to you. You must behave like a Jeckyll and Hyde, showing aggressive behaviour when the dog ignores you and submissive behaviour (crouching, soft voice) the instant it looks at you or shows some interest. Some dogs will come after the first throw, but you may have to throw your chain twenty to thirty times, depending on your dog's responsiveness. You won't know until you start, but do not quit until the dog comes to you. Repeat this training for a week on a daily basis until your dog has become very reliable. Do not allow your pet off the lead in other areas until you are confident it will obey you on the first command.

Lead Training

To train your dog to walk correctly on a lead you must first of all accustom it to the check chain or collar and lead. Most pups will scratch at their neck if they have not been used to wearing a collar. You can liken it to when your first put on a watch; you are aware of it on your wrist, but after some time you become so accustomed to it that if it fell off you would not notice. So give your dog a little time to adjust. Once your dog is used to its collar, attach a light lead and allow the dog to drag the lead along the ground. Some distractions (such as food) might be necessary during this time as your dog might be a bit concerned about the lead.

Do not allow your dog to bite the lead at all. This might look cute but you may have to live with this behaviour for the rest of your dog's life if you let it occur. It will also cost you a fortune in chewed leads. Also do not leave your dog unattended during this time, as the lead may become snagged and distress the dog, something which it could then associate with the lead.

Once your dog is happy with its lead and collar, pick up the end of the lead. Let your dog take you for a walk and, while allowing it to feel some resistance, let it lead you wherever it wants. Once you are convinced your dog is comfortable with the lead, then take control. While the dog

Train your dog always to come up to your left side when it is on the lead. If the dog pulls or wanders, crouch down and call the dog to you, praising it when it comes to your side. If the dog pulls, snap back the lead and say 'Bah'.

is pulling ahead, stop and crouch down. In a soft, melodic voice say, 'Come on, good puppy, good dog'. If your dog resists you, pat your legs, still crouching, and praise it when it comes to your side. Now step off again, then crouch down and pat your legs once more if it starts to pull away. You want your dog to come up on your left side. Keep going in this manner until it walks easily by your side, praising it each time it does so. Do not allow your dog to pull ahead. Snap back with the lead each time your pet pulls on it and say 'Bah'. Praise your dog every time it comes back to your side.

Heel On-Lead

This training should be commenced in your backyard. Use the check chain and the 2 metre (6 foot) lead. The check chain should be loose and the lead should be distinctly slack when your dog is walking by your side. Your dog should always be walked on your left side, and its front legs should be level with your legs. Praise your dog in a soft voice and fondle your dog's head when it's in the correct position. Continue walking in this manner, saying 'Bah' each time your dog steps out of position, snapping the lead and then praising the instant it steps back into line.

To check your dog, snap the lead tight and release it immediately. To do this correctly, first loosen the check

To train your dog to heel on the lead, use the check chain and a 2 metre (6 foot) lead. The dog should be trained to walk on your left, keeping its front legs level with your legs. Praise the dog when it walks correctly, but snap the lead and say 'Bah' when it does not.

chain slightly by moving the hand holding the lead towards the dog, then tug it quickly backwards and loosen it again. This makes the metallic sound we want. Whenever your dog is pulling ahead or lagging behind, say 'Bah', checking at the same time.

If your dog tries to cross to the wrong (right) side, just snap the lead and reprimand it. As soon as the dog comes back to the correct side, praise it. Remember that dogs are natural pullers, so keep the lead slack and keep the dog on its best behaviour by reprimanding it consistently.

Difficult Dogs
A dog that refuses to walk properly on the lead can be cured by using one of the following methods:

1. Take your dog to a strange area and put it on the lead. Ask a helper to hold the dog, then walk about 30 paces away. Call your dog and crouch down. Ask the helper to walk with your dog towards you, mildly restricting it by holding the lead back, but repeatedly saying 'Come on' until they reach you. Practise this several times over a period of a few days. Eventually the dog will walk forward on its own when you say 'Come on'. Once the

dog is walking well, stop it if it pulls by snapping its check chain back and releasing quickly while you say 'Bah'.

2. Place your dog on a lead. With a piece of diced chicken or something equally as tempting held in your right hand, hold the lead in your left hand and say 'Come on'. Bring the food close to the dog's nose, then forward again to encourage the dog to take a few steps. Praise it when it does. Keep repeating 'Come on' over and over again; this is what your dog will eventually have to respond to once you stop using the food incentive. When your pet takes a few forward steps, give it the food and praise it, then make the dog walk a little further each time before its next reward. Once your dog is walking properly on its lead, use the check chain to stop it from pulling and discontinue the food. The food not only provides a good distraction from the lead, but will actually give the dog fond memories of it.

The Sit

The easiest way to get your dog to sit is on-lead. All your training should be on-lead initially, since without it you lose control. Place the dog on your left. With your right hand, grasp the lead close to the dog's neck and press gently down on its rump with your left hand, checking at the same time. Repeat the word 'Sit' as you do this. Allow the lead to slacken and remove your hand from the dog's rump once it sits. Say 'Bah' if the dog moves, the instant it moves. Praise in a soft voice as soon as you are able to get your dog to do this without hopping straight back up.

The Drop or Down

I prefer to use the word 'Drop' as the command for this exercise, because it's not generally used in our everyday conversation. Where possible, I have selected commands from words we seldom use. This way the dog won't be as easily confused.

To train your dog to sit, hold the lead close to the dog's neck in your right hand and press down on its rump with your left, repeating the word 'Sit'. Remove your hand and praise the dog when it sits correctly, but say 'Bah' if it moves from the sit without command.

Sit.

CASE HISTORY: A gentleman I was tutoring with his Rottweiler had chosen to use the word 'okay' whenever he wished his dog to go free. This worked well until I was giving the owner instructions regarding training. Each time I spoke, the man would answer 'okay', and the dog would immediately jump up from the stay.

With the dog standing on your left side, hold all the lead in your left hand. Next, place your left hand on the dog's back just behind the dog's shoulder blades while at the same time putting your right hand on its muzzle. This should be done in the following way: place your middle finger and index finger in an inverted 'V' on the dog's muzzle, your palm covering its eyes (see diagram on the next page). Then, press firmly but gently in a downward motion with both hands, releasing the pressure as soon as your dog starts to go down. Remember to repeat 'Drop' as you do this. Your dog has no idea of what you are trying to do but if you praise your dog as soon as it drops down, it will soon catch on. If the dog tries to fight you, say 'Bah' and start again. Be patient and do not lose your temper.

Your dog must also learn to wait for the 'Free' command

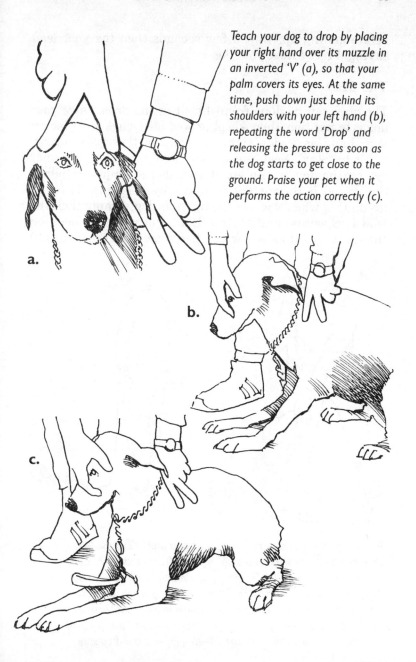

Teach your dog to drop by placing your right hand over its muzzle in an inverted 'V' (a), so that your palm covers its eyes. At the same time, push down just behind its shoulders with your left hand (b), repeating the word 'Drop' and releasing the pressure as soon as the dog starts to get close to the ground. Praise your pet when it performs the action correctly (c).

a.

b.

c.

before getting up. Wait a few seconds then tug your lead saying 'Free'. Praise your dog.

The Stay

The stay can be done from the sit or the drop. Once your dog is in position, then, keeping your lead slack and placing your hand as a stop signal in front of the dog's muzzle, tell it to 'Stay'. Next, move away two paces, keeping your eye on the dog as you go. If your dog attempts to follow, reprimand it the instant it moves by checking its chain (to do this when you are facing your dog, simply flick the lead backwards) and saying 'Bah'. Put your dog back on the exact spot it moved from, then repeat the exercise until

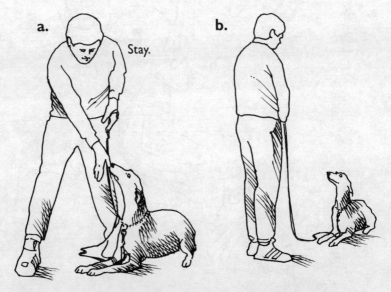

To teach your dog to stay, put it into a sit or a drop. Keep the lead slack and hold your hand in a 'stop' signal in front of its muzzle and repeat the word 'Stay' (a). Keeping your eyes on the dog, take two steps away. Reprimand the dog if it moves from position, but praise it when it responds (b). The dog should remain in place until you say 'Free'. Gradually build up the time your dog is made to stay from 30 seconds to 5 minutes for a sit and 10–20 minutes for a drop stay.

it stays. Leave your dog in that position for 30 seconds to start with, then gradually build up the time over a period of two weeks. Build to 5 minutes for the sit and 10 to 20 minutes for the drop. Always make sure the lead has a clear amount of slack to it.

Once your dog has stayed the desired length of time, return to it, wait a couple of seconds and say 'Free'. (If you release your dog the instant you return, it will start to anticipate and therefore move the second you return.) Praise it lavishly. Let your dog think it's done something wonderful. It is not a good idea to pat your dog during the stay as this will distract it. Just praise it verbally until you free it from the stay.

KEY POINTS

- **Language:** Your dog does not understand our language, so you must teach it. Therefore, keep your communication basic; use single words, not sentences.

- **Programming:** Programme your dog to the 'Bah' word first.

- **Timing:** In order for your dog to catch on to what you want, your timing must be precise. The most desirable situation is to catch your dog in the act of doing something wrong.

- **Reprimands:** Your dog must receive a substantial reprimand when it does something wrong.

- **Reprisals:** Never punish your dog for something it has previously done by dragging it back to the scene.

- **Punishment:** Do not use a rolled-up newspaper or a stick to punish your dog. In most cases, using a harsh tone, Bah, and the throw chain to reinforce it will be all you need. In extreme conditions, use the lead reprimand (lifting your dog off its front paws on the lead).

- **Praise:** Be sure to praise your dog lavishly each time it does what you want.

▶ PART TWO ◀

HOW TO SOLVE YOUR DOG'S SPECIFIC BEHAVIOURAL PROBLEMS

As well as basic training, your dog may require special attention to solve its specific behavioural problems. As with people, no dog is perfect all the time. Right now your dog may be exhibiting specific problems, such as barking, biting or digging in the garden; or these problems may develop at some time in the future, maybe because you have had to leave your dog in someone else's care. The remainder of this book is therefore devoted to solving specific behavioural problems in your dog. But first there are a few techniques I find useful to achieve the most effective results. (And remember, for all cures your dog must already be programmed to the word 'Bah'.)

▶ CHAPTER THREE ◀

Reprimand Techniques

The techniques you can use to reprimand your dog are many and varied. The two most recommended in this book (the throw chain method and the water method, both combined with 'Bah') can be made even more effective when some strong discipline is required. One method in particular, scene setting, is useful in many problem-solving situations.

Another method, the strong reprimand, is very effective in reinforcing the throw chain reprimand, but it should only be used as a special programming technique and not as a part of general problem solving.

As I have already mentioned, the forms of reprimand outlined in this book should not be used to punish your dog; they are, first, ways of letting your dog know that you are the leader and therefore to be obeyed; and second, a means of communicating with your dog to let it know what you want. As always, when your dog does catch on and begins to behave well, praise it lavishly to let it know you are pleased with it.

THE THROW CHAIN METHOD

This is by far the easiest and most effective of all methods and will work on approximately 90 per cent of dogs. See page 25 if you need to refresh your memory on how to use the throw chain correctly.

THE WATER METHOD

Fill a water sprayer with water, and spray your dog in the face at the precise moment it is doing something wrong. Praise your dog the instant it stops misbehaving.

SCENE SETTING

Scene setting simply means making things happen when you want them to. You, or yourself and a helper, set up the situation in which the dog is likely to misbehave, so that you can catch it in the act to make your reprimand most effective.

CASE HISTORY: A bull terrier always barked at one particular neighbour. Even though the owner had the neighbour feed the dog, pat it and make friends, as soon as the neighbour would go into his own yard, the dog would bark savagely at him. So I was called in.

As luck would have it, the next-door neighbour was only too pleased to help with the dog's therapy, so we set the scene. The dog's owner pretended to go to work, driving his car up the road and around the corner. He then walked back, sneaked into his neighbour's yard and hid behind him as he entered the front garden. As soon as the dog began to bark at the neighbour, the owner popped out and threw a throw chain near the dog, saying 'Bah' at the same time. The dog was reprimanded at the instant it misbehaved and, in this way, quickly cured.

With scene setting you can cure a dog much faster because, with a concentrated effort, the dog will receive the reprimand until it stops doing the wrong thing. Without scene setting, you would only be able to reprimand your dog when you could see (or hear) it misbehaving.

STRONG-REPRIMAND TECHNIQUE

This is what you can use if all the previous methods prove unsuccessful. You will need to tie your dog up in a garage or shed, somewhere where the sound of the throw chain will be amplified. Throw the chain at the wall a couple of times, yelling 'Bah', until you get a reaction from your dog.

There are very few dogs that need this strong-reinforcement programming, as most dogs quit easily with the basic methods. The strong-reprimand technique is mostly used in situations where the amplification of the sound from the throw chain is deadened, for example, by the grassy surface of a paddock (as in 'Stock Chasing' on page 110).

SNAPPY TRAINER

The Snappy Trainer is a handy training aid, available from your local vet. This ingenious little device, which resembles a mouse trap but comes without the risk that a conventional mouse trap brings, works on the startle factor — a paddle smacks the dog on the nose.

The correct-sized paddle can be bought to suit the size of your dog (or cat). It can be effective in discouraging the dog that attacks the washing, or steals food from benches and garbage bins. In such cases, it could be considered an alternative to the methods suggested in this book.

ASKING OTHER PEOPLE TO REPRIMAND YOUR DOG

If you ever ask anybody else to reprimand your dog, first make sure the dog respects the authority of that person, otherwise it may become aggressive. I would never go into any dog's territory and just expect it to obey me: I would discipline the dog first by programming it, otherwise it could seek to reprimand me for my impertinence at challenging its authority.

With some dogs, having another person give the reprimand won't be a problem, especially if the dog already knows and respects that person. However, it may sometimes be necessary for programming to occur first, with the owner present to ensure that the dog remains well behaved. If the dog does become aggressive, put it on a lead so that you can stay in control of the situation. There are some dogs that just won't be dominated by someone other than their owner (see the case history on page 107). Whatever the circumstances, responsibility for a dog's behaviour always rests with the owner.

▶ CHAPTER FOUR ◀

Common Problems

Most of the cures discussed in this chapter deal with one basic problem: aggression. If your dog is displaying some form of aggressive behaviour, it needs to be dealt with quickly and cured before any other problems your dog might have, such as digging in the garden.

BARKING BACK AT YOUR COMMANDS

If your dog has no respect for you, it will more than likely answer back, barking at you when you reprimand it, just like a naughty child. If your dog is in the habit of doing this, or if it starts to do this, do not condone it. The moment your dog starts to answer back, pick up a throw chain, go after the dog and throw the chain again and again in conjunction with 'Bah' until the dog stops misbehaving. Praise your dog the instant this happens. It usually only takes one or two of these outbursts from you to cure your dog of answering back.

AGGRESSION

Aggression from your dog towards you or any member of your family should *never* be tolerated. If you allow your dog to bite without any retaliation from you, then you are placing yourself and others in danger. A man in England was attacked by his dog when he tried to go near it when it was eating. The dog attacked him so savagely that he bled to death before anyone could get to him. I don't wish to scare you unnecessarily, but I feel very strongly about dogs being aggressive towards their owners because I know what it can lead to.

Dogs that attack their owners or other people are often put to sleep. They are presumed to be psychologically unstable because the owner is unable to understand why a well-loved pet should behave in such a way. Viciousness in dogs should not be tolerated, but many dogs meet an untimely end simply because they were acting like dogs; that is, acting according to the pecking order of the group in which they live. For a dog to behave as its owners wish, it must perceive them as the dominant members of its social group whose rules are to be obeyed. Treat your dog like a dog (and not like a human), otherwise it will more than likely not respect you and not obey your commands.

Dogs can be a lethal weapon, and an attack from your dog on another person can have serious repercussions: not only could the dog be put down, but you could be prosecuted. As well as training your dog, make sure that people can come into your property with safety. Visitors and meter readers, among others, need to be able to enter your yard without fear of being attacked.

Many people think that although their dog behaves aggressively, for example, growling from time to time, it does not really mean it. I cannot stress enough how wrong this opinion is. Aggressive behaviour is undesirable and can escalate; a growl from a dog is a warning that if you keep doing a certain thing, the dog will bite.

All aggression must be nipped in the bud. If you have not got the heart for it, then seek expert help.

The cure you employ with this particular behavioural problem will depend on why your dog behaves aggressively. If your dog behaves in an unpredictable way — if it is friendly one minute and aggressive the next — it will be hard for you to predict when you may need to be ready to reprimand it. All you can do is carry your throw chain or water sprayer whenever you are with the dog so that you can reprimand it with 'Bah' and the throw chain or water sprayer as soon as it behaves aggressively. Praise your dog the instant it behaves. Alternatively, you could monitor your dog's behaviour to work out when your dog behaves aggressively — and what situations trigger it. You could then leave a lead attached to the dog during those times you suspect it would be most likely to attack you or growl, and simply lift the dog's front paws off the ground for a couple of seconds and say 'Bah'.

Be very determined. Do not think the problem will disappear if you do not persevere. If you believe this then you might as well put the lead on yourself and give the dog full control. You will have lost the battle. Programming your dog daily helps to prevent aggressive behaviour because it reinforces your dominance over the dog (see the final point in 'Key Points', page 112). I strongly urge you not to overlook any form of aggression from your dog, no matter how trivial it might seem.

CASE HISTORY: Max, a four-year-old German shepherd, was dearly loved by his owners. He, in turn, never showed anything but good behaviour towards them. He lived with a family whose fourteen-year-old son loved Max. He and the dog went everywhere together. Unlike his mum and dad, Daniel did not believe in reprimanding Max because he felt the dog would not like him anymore if he did so. One day Max was in the yard chewing on a stick when Daniel came to take him for his walk. Max attacked the boy when he tried to pick up the stick, ripping his face so that he needed five stitches.

Daniel's father called me because no one could work out why the dog had turned nasty and he was considering having Max put down. I explained to him that the dog is a pack animal and, as such, follows certain instincts: it is the boss over any other dog in the pack that it can dominate; it is the subordinate of any other dog that can dominate it.

Dogs look upon humans as members of the pack. The dog had no intention of maiming Daniel; it was reprimanding him in much the same way as it would reprimand another dog further down the pecking order. (Dogs, with their loose-fitting skin and protective covering of fur, are far more equipped to withstand a bite from another dog than we are with our tight-fitting skin that rips easily.)

Remonstrance, not vicious injury, would have been Max's intention.

I did feel that the situation could happen again, unless Daniel showed more dominance over the dog. The only way to achieve this, other than having an all-out physical battle with the pet, was through obedience training in which the dog would learn to respect Daniel more so that it would no longer be game to attack.

POSSESSIVENESS

If your dog becomes possessive of an object — for example, a chair or toy — and then is aggressive when you try to take the object from it, use either your water sprayer or throw chain and 'Bah' to reprimand the dog. A very determined dog should probably be put on a lead. Leave the lead trailing on the ground and attempt to take the object, each time reprimanding any aggressive behaviour by lifting your dog's front paws off the ground for a couple of seconds and saying 'Bah'. Praise your dog as soon as it stops its aggressive behaviour.

Possessiveness of People

CASE HISTORY: A female poodle, owned by a couple, had become very attached to the male owner — so much so that whenever it saw the man kiss or cuddle his wife, it would bark at them until they stopped. The couple were in a quandary as to how to fix the problem, so called me in.

I told the man to give the dog something pleasant to eat (its favourite treat) the next time he kissed his wife. In this way the dog would come to associate the kissing and cuddling with a good experience. With repeated effort (and some treats later) the dog was cured.

It is up to the person whom the dog is being possessive of to reprimand the pet whenever it steps out of line with other people. If your dog isn't keen on its food, then use the throw chain with 'Bah' to reprimand the dog. Always praise your dog the instant it stops misbehaving.

Possessiveness of Food

Dogs are, by nature, very protective of their food. Their survival in the wild depends on it. How long would a wild dog survive if it just allowed any animal to steal its food? We have to teach the dog that we have no intention of stealing its food.

If you can't go near your dog while it is eating, you have a big problem. Not only is it dangerous for you, but also extremely dangerous for any children that may live in the house or visit you. Under no circumstances should you tolerate this from your dog.

When clients tell me that their dog becomes aggressive when it has a bone, but that they simply leave it alone while it's eating, I ask 'What if the dog, unbeknown to you, buries something in the garden and you or one of your children unsuspectingly goes near that spot or digs the

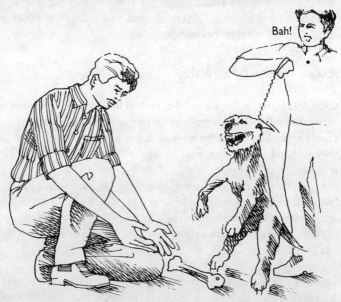

Bah!

If your dog behaves possessively about food, place it on a lead then give the dog a large bone. Move to take the bone away and if your pet growls or snaps, lift its front feet off the ground briefly, saying 'Bah'.

object up? The dog could launch a vicious attack to protect its food'. This is not fantasy. I have heard of cases where such attacks from dogs were so vicious that the owners lost their lives. Aggression while eating is serious business; do not view it lightly. Yet, there is no need to take drastic measures since the problem is curable.

If you have a puppy that is possessive of its food, then the cure will be fairly swift. Place your pup on a lead and check chain, and give it a large bone. Wait until the pup is chewing away happily, then move in. Pick up the end of the lead, take hold of the bone and say 'Give'. If your pup growls or shows aggression, however minor, reprimand by saying 'Bah' and shaking the lead violently. From here, there's no turning back. You must keep going, no matter how long it takes, until your pup happily gives up its bone. Once that happens, praise your pet lavishly.

Be sure to keep control of the pup with the lead, and do not allow it to crawl away with the bone to stop you from taking it. Never take a bone that you do not intend giving back, and make sure your pup always gets the bone back each time it stops its aggressive behaviour and allows you to pick up the bone.

You may need to go through the same routine every time you feed your pup. Eventually, however, it will quite happily accept that whenever you take its bone, if it waits patiently, you will give it back. The dog's motivation to become aggressive will disappear when it realises that you are not going to steal its food. If you own a puppy, let it get used to you being nearby when it's eating by taking, and returning, its food. This will help prevent future food possessiveness problems.

If you have a fully grown dog that is being possessive of its food, again, place it on a lead so that you can stay in control of the situation. Give your dog a large bone, then pick up the end of the lead and move in as though you are going to take the bone. If your dog growls or snaps, lift it off its front legs for a couple of seconds only, say 'Bah', then try again. A very large or difficult to handle dog, can be effectively dealt with by looping its lead over a rotary clothes line. You could also ask a friend or another family member to help you lift the dog when it growls at you.

Important: When doing any of this training, keep your own and your dog's safety uppermost in your mind. Do not lose your temper; it must be a controlled situation — and keep well clear of snapping teeth! Only hold your dog off the ground for a couple of seconds, until your dog stops behaving badly. If you stop too soon, the dog will only be more aggressive next time. Should this training prove too difficult for you, seek professional help.

PLAYFULLY BITING YOUR FINGERS

A dog tends to use its mouth for almost everything. Biting is usually more prominent in a dominant pup or dog, and in the dog that is trying to dominate *you* (as mentioned earlier, a dog from lower down the pack may exhibit dominant behaviour if it perceives you as being even lower in the pack than it). Licking, on the other hand, indicates a submissive dog. Biting can be encouraged by bad handling or games where you stick your hands in the dog's

If your dog bites or chews on your fingers, never pull your hand away. Instead, spray the dog in the face with the water sprayer, saying 'Bah' as you do. Praise it as soon as it releases your hand.

Bah!

mouth. Children tend to be the biggest offenders of this latter type of behaviour and should not be encouraged to play with a dog in this way.

To cure this problem, try your water sprayer first. Spray your dog in the face each time it bites your fingers or hand. Always leave the hand your dog is biting totally still, and spray with the other hand. Do not pull your hand away because this action only removes the object your dog is getting into trouble for biting and it will not catch on that it should never bite any hand, whether close to its mouth or not. Your dog must be in the action of biting your hand when you spray it and say 'Bah'. You could also smear your hands with mustard to give the dog an unpleasant taste each time it bites your hand. This may be messy, but it works very well. Finally, if all else fails, use your throw chain at your dog's feet and say 'Bah', then praise it the instant it stops biting.

BITING YOUR ANKLES OR CLOTHING

Use your throw chain for this one. Wait for your dog to grab your clothing or ankles then, while you are standing still, throw the chain and say 'Bah'. Praise your dog, saying 'Good boy' or 'Good girl', the instant it stops biting.

DOGS AND CHILDREN

Dogs and children are great together. They seem to be a natural combination. However, problems can and do arise, and dogs must be shown that our children are precious to us and that under no circumstances must they step over the line.

Statistics show that a large number of the children attacked by dogs are between the ages of two and five years old. A big percentage of these children are either bitten by their own dog or that of a friend or relative. My theory is that a dog relates to children as though they were puppies. In a pack situation, dogs are very protective of their pups since the other dogs may perceive a pup as a potential threat to its position in the pack and attack it. A pack leader would attack any dog that hurt its pups, so if you want your dog to respect your children, you must have the same control as a pack leader.

You should also make sure the children do not over-step the mark themselves, by, for example, teasing the dog or pulling its ears and tail. Children should be taught from an early age that dogs can feel pain, just like we can, and that they are not inanimate objects like dolls or teddy bears. Leaving your dog and child playing in the backyard is rather like leaving two children playing in the backyard — sooner or later they will fall out with each other. The only difference is that the dog will lash out with its teeth; the child gets bitten, and, as a sad consequence, the dog may be put down. All the dog did was 'smack' the child, perhaps even because the child smacked it first.

CASE HISTORY: The story of an adoring Great Dane pops into my mind when I think of dogs and children. The Dane's greatest mate was an eleven-year-old boy. One day, the boy had a friend over to the house, while his mum was out. The two boys were playing rough, wrestling each other, when the dog, thinking his mate was under attack, lunged at the visitor. He bit him so severely that the child ended up in hospital. This was another case of a dog acting instinctively but acting against the human code. In this situation, the dog was not destroyed but returned to the breeder.

When we leave children and dogs together, we have no way of knowing what might happen or what the children might do that will cause the dog to act in a way we might not expect.

I do not condone leaving children and dogs together unattended. I know many readers will argue that their dog and children have played together happily for years. I do not doubt they have. Some dogs, such as those which exhibit bottom-of-the-pack behaviour or more dominant dogs which are well disciplined, will never bite or reprimand children. But previous behaviour is no guarantee for the future.

Prevent any unfortunate incidents occurring when dogs and children play together by supervising them constantly. Always insist that the dog understands that the children are to be given precedence.

I remember a newspaper reporting an incident in which a dog had attacked and killed a baby boy — even though the dog had been brought up with the owners' other children and had never shown any signs of aggression during that time. You just never know what a dog will do. The dog may have perceived the child as a threat to its position in the family (the pack). Both the dog and the child were male — this could have been an influencing factor.

In my profession, I hear many stories about dog attacks on children that do not make the newspapers. But, with training and supervision, these situations can be avoided — just like a pack leader, we need to protect our young.

What to do where dogs and children are concerned

1. The dog should not be allowed to knock the child over without receiving a reprimand.

2. The dog should not be allowed to steal objects such as food, toys, balls, and so on, from the child.

3. A child must always precede the dog through any door or gate. The dog must always wait until the child has entered the house or yard first.

4. Children should not be allowed to reprimand the dog; they do not have enough authority to dominate the animal and may be bitten in the power struggle. You must reprimand the dog for the child.

5. Children and dogs should never be left together without supervision, even if training has occurred. Never under any circumstances leave a baby on the ground or alone with a dog.

Points 1 to 3 establish a position of greater authority of the child over the dog. Points 4 and 5 stop situations arising in which this authority would be undermined.

TAIL CHASING

An otherwise normal dog can become quite obsessive about chasing its tail. The problem usually develops because the dog has no idea that the object it can see swishing around behind it is part of its own body. This often happens when the colour of the dog's tail (or the colour of the tip of the tail) is a different colour to the rest of the dog. The dog turns to grab the object (its tail), the tail moves when the dog does, and the chase is on. Another cause for the problem is boredom. Tail chasing commonly begins when a dog is very young, bored and looking for a bit of fun. Once started, this problem can make a dog appear quite mad.

If your dog chases its tail, check the colour of the tail compared to the rest of the dog. If it is a different colour, the solution is to dye the tail to match the rest of the dog's coat or to cover the tail with some suitably coloured material. If dyeing is an option, seek professional advice from your vet as to how to go about it.

Alternatively, if there is no colour variation on your dog but it is still chasing its tail, you can use the throw chain reprimand to cure this habit. Wait for your dog to start chasing its tail, then throw the throw chain near its back legs and say 'Bah' at the same time. Keep repeating this procedure until the dog is cured. If your dog fails to respond to the throw chain, place it on a lead and wait until your pet starts to chase its tail, then say 'Bah' and yank the lead upwards shaking it vigorously until it stops its chasing. It may take several efforts to cure the dog of its bad habit, but persevere and always remember to praise your dog the instant it stops chasing its tail.

THE MOST COMMON PROBLEM: BARKING

It is not wise (or peaceful!) to let your dog bark at everything that moves. A good guard dog should let you know when a stranger is entering your property, not when they are several blocks away or even walking past the front of the house. And they should not bark at dogs, birds, cats, falling leaves or neighbours either.

To control unwarranted barking, be sure to catch your dog in the act. Sneak up and throw your throw chain near the dog's feet or bounce them off a fence or a tin shed and say 'Bah'. Praise your dog the instant it stops barking.

For details on how to cure specific barking problems, see the many relevant sections in the following chapters.

▶ CHAPTER FIVE ◀

Yard Problems

This section of the book is designed to help solve problems you may be having with your dog in the backyard.

JUMPING UP

This is a very common problem and frequently begins when the dog is young. The puppy, in view of its size, is encouraged by its owners to jump up so that they don't have to bend down. The pup's bad habit then continues into adulthood. It is not wise to let your pup do anything that will become a problem when it is fully grown.

To cure this problem it is essential that you make the experience as unpleasant as possible for your dog when it is jumping on you, and as pleasant as possible when it has stopped.

There are three different methods to use to cure the problem of jumping up.

The Knee and Foot Action Method

Each time the dog jumps on you, bring your knee up between you and the dog and say 'Bah', while at the same time pushing your dog away with your knee. Do not use your hands, put them behind your back and stand totally still; the more you swing and move your body, the more your dog will jump about. Freeze the action as soon as your dog jumps, bending only your knee to push the dog away.

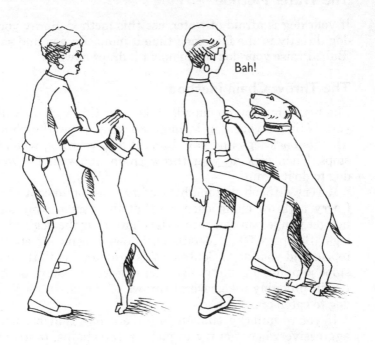

Bah!

WRONG **RIGHT**

Never use your hands or move around a lot when you are trying to teach a dog not to jump up: these actions will only encourage it (left). Instead, stand still, put your hands behind your back and bend your knee to push the dog away, saying 'Bah'. As soon as the dog drops to the ground praise it.

As soon as your dog's paws hit the ground, praise it, but say 'Bah' again the instant it jumps back up on you.

Some dogs, when cured of jumping on you from the front, will run around the back and try the same there. If this happens, do not turn around. Bend your knee and kick your heel up behind you so that it connects with the dog, saying 'Bah' as you do. Remember to freeze the action. Praise your dog the instant it behaves.

The Water Method

If your dog is afraid of water, use this method. Spray your dog directly in the face each time it jumps on you and say 'Bah'. Praise your dog the moment it drops down.

The Throw Chain Method

The next time you go outside, take your throw chain with you. Wait for your dog to jump on you, throw the chain near its back legs and say 'Bah'. Praise your dog when it stops. Then pick up your throw chain and wait for your dog to do it again.

A very difficult dog might need two people to control it. Carry a throw chain each, so that the person who does not get jumped on can throw the chain near the dog's hind legs. (See page 50 for details on allowing someone else to reprimand your dog.) Continue this procedure until the dog stops jumping up, and praise your dog when it stays down. It will probably take several throws of the chain for your dog to catch on.

If you're unlucky enough to have a dog that becomes aggressive when you try to pick up the chains, overcome this by tying a piece of lightweight rope on your chains, so that you can pick them up without bending down, which puts you in a vulnerable position. Alternatively, have several sets of throw chains. If the dog continues to behave aggressively, put it on-lead and then give the dog a shake and say 'Bah' as you continue the training. The lead will help you to stay in control of the situation. Of course, seek professional help if there is ever any risk to your safety or if the dog isn't responding.

RUSHING THROUGH A GATE OR A DOOR

A dog that rushes into the house or rushes out of the yard every time you open the back door or side gate can be a real nuisance.

To cure your dog of this bad habit put it on a lead, making sure the lead is slack. Next, open the back door, wait for

Never allow your dog to push through a gate in front of you. To train it to wait at an open gate, attach the long lead to a post and to the dog's collar. This will stop it running off. Walk through the gate and yell 'Bah' and check the dog back behind the gate if it attempts to follow. If it stays, praise it.

The next step is to surprise the dog with your sudden appearance. This will ensure that the training works in all situations. Keep the dog attached to the post on the long lead. Hide, and then step out suddenly. If the dog rushes towards you through the gate, yell 'Bah' and throw the chain near its feet. Praise the dog for good behaviour.

the dog to rush into the house, then snap the lead back and say 'Bah'. It is even better to place the lead on the ground, allowing freedom of movement, and then stand on it at the last moment just before your dog charges in.

Once you are sure the dog understands what is expected, repeat the exercise, but this time with you inside the house and the dog outside. Open the door a fraction, blocking the entrance with your body. If your dog attempts to enter, say 'Bah'. (If your dog has been successfully programmed to the 'Bah' reprimand, it should respond.) If your dog pushes past you into the house, grab the lead and yell 'Bah'. Put your dog back outside.

When your dog no longer tries to push past you, the next step is to take its lead off, keeping the throw chain handy to throw in the dog's path if it attempts to enter. At this stage of the training, close all the internal doors to avoid a mad chase through the house. Remember, praise your dog when it obeys you.

To stop your dog rushing through any garden gates, use an extra long lead and anchor it to the fence. Stand beside your dog, open the gate and wait for the dog to rush through it. Stand on the lead and say 'Bah' the instant this happens. Keep reprimanding your dog in this way until it stops rushing through.

Next, step through the gate yourself, and yell 'Bah' if your dog attempts to follow. You might need your throw chain or water sprayer if you have a determined dog. Once your dog realises you do not want it to follow you, add the element of surprise. Hide out of your dog's sight, but be sure you can step into view quickly. Your dog should still, at this stage, be tied to a long, lightweight lead attached to the fence. Have your throw chain ready to use in conjunction with 'Bah' if your dog attempts to go through the open gate.

It is not advisable to leave the gate open for long periods and expect your dog not to go through. This exercise is only designed for those times when you have to take something like a lawnmower or pushbike through the gate and you do not wish your dog to get out. After about a week's training, your dog should stop going through the gate when it's off the lead.

FENCE JUMPING

This is a very bad behavioural problem and one which is very difficult to cure, making prevention a much better option. The problem occurs because the yard in which the dog is kept is insecure; the dog can escape easily, either by jumping over a low fence or by pushing its way through or under a weak fence. Once the dog learns there is a way out, it won't quit trying to escape no matter how strong or high you build the fence. Make sure you have adequate fencing, secure enough to hold your pup or dog, before it arrives. Check your fence properly by kicking and pushing it forcefully, the way a dog would. If your fence is inadequate in parts, do not put a dog in the yard. Wait until you can secure it properly, otherwise you will have a frustrating life chasing a dog that won't stay where it's put. The RSPCA spends many hours checking the premises of prospective buyers of its dogs to ensure that they are going to secure yards.

If you own a dog that keeps escaping your yard, there are very few things you can try. One is to catch your dog in the act of jumping over the fence. If you manage this, use your throw chain so that it lands right at the top of the fence the moment your dog's head appears, or throw a bucket of water over the fence. With both methods say 'Bah' and try to catch your dog by surprise. These shock tactics usually work with a young, impressionable dog but are unlikely to work with an older one because it's almost impossible to predict exactly where a notorious 'escapee' is likely to jump over. You might catch the dog going over one particular part of the fence, but that won't necessarily stop it from trying somewhere else.

If all else fails, you could try altering your fence in such a way as to make it impossible for your dog to get out by placing 90-degree angle bars spaced along the top of your

Fence jumping is a difficult problem to cure because the dog must be caught in the act.
One training method is to throw a bucket of water at the dog as soon as its face appears over the fence. Yell 'Bah' at the same time. Try to take your dog by surprise.

fence so that they point back into your yard (rather than adding height), then running a rope or wire along these. Another method would be to place upright bars above the fence and run string along them, making the fence higher. You will only need these constructions until the dog gives up its bad habit. The results you get will depend on how long your dog has been jumping over the fence and how determined it is to keep trying.

If none of the above methods are successful, then perhaps a completely enclosed pen with a concrete floor and mesh roof might be the only way you can keep your pet safe. Make sure your dog gets plenty of exercise if it is kept in a pen; take it for lots of walks. If penning is your only option, however, barking might suddenly become a new problem (see section on barking, page 83).

CHEWING

Chewing is a natural activity for your young pup or dog. Just as a teething baby likes to chew on something firm, a pup likes to do the same. It becomes a problem when the pup or dog gnaws on something you don't want it to, for example, shoes or furniture. Fortunately there are some things you can do to substantially reduce your pup's chewing habit. As well as the method discussed in 'Protecting Your Possessions', below, you can put your pup in a playpen. Then, when you are unable to watch it, you can control its environment by only putting into the pen those things you want your pup to chew, such as rusks or bones.

Stress also plays a big part in how much a dog will chew. We really do not know how much stress we put our poor dogs through each time we leave them alone. Dogs are pack animals and expect that when the rest of the pack leaves the house they should follow. A dog that is deprived of the company of its owner for long periods of time is likely to suffer from stress, and chewing might result.

A pen is the safest and most hassle-free way to keep your puppy in its early years. Once you are sure the chewing has stopped, then your dog can be allowed more freedom. Remember to give a penned dog lots of exercise and training.

CASE HISTORY: My husband's German shepherd, Cinta, was very well behaved and rarely chewed, until the time my husband went to hospital for a week. My husband returned home, and immediately went out to greet his dog who was delighted to see him. Unfortunately, he had to leave again on business right away. When he returned home three hours later, Cinta had demolished our wooden verandah; she had chewed every bit of railing she could find. The stress of seeing her beloved owner for only a few seconds after he had been away for so long, and then to have him whisked away again, upset her too much.

Protecting Your Possessions

Although chewing is a natural activity for pups, your possessions are precious. You can protect your garden furniture and so on by painting it with something that will taste unpleasant, such as hot chilli sauce. This simple procedure ensures that your pup or dog will be 'repri-manded' the instant it begins to chew.

Be sure to pick up everything lying around such as shoes, plant pots and precious items and put them away. You can bring them back out when the dog is older. You cannot expect a pup to know what it can or cannot touch. Anything is fair game, especially something which has its owner's scent on it.

PULLING THE WASHING OFF THE LINE

The best way to cure this bad habit is to let the washing line reprimand the dog. I know that sounds silly, but I'll explain.

Select five old pillow cases, cover the bottom of them with a layer of very hot pepper and peg them securely on the line, low enough for your dog to reach them. When the dog

An effective method of teaching your dog not to pull washing off the line is to sprinkle a layer of cayenne pepper into the bottom of five old pillow cases and attach them to the clothes line low enough for the dog to reach them. The pepper provides an immediate deterrent.

pulls at the washing, it receives the unpleasant taste of the pepper as an immediate reprimand.

Chronic washing-pullers can be cured by putting cactus plant leaves in the pillow cases. Leave the pillow cases out for about one week, replenishing the filling from time-to-time. Do not put any of your own washing out during this time. Your dog must learn that anything it touches on the line will give it an unpleasant experience.

DIGGING

Dogs are natural diggers: they dig burrows in the wild to provide protection from heat and cold; and a bitch digs herself a lair in which to give birth to her puppies and to provide protection. Dogs also dig to bury their food, preserving it for later. Over-feeding a dog or giving it large bones may trigger its digging instinct. If your dog buries its food, check that it is not for these reasons before you begin any of the cures given here. Keep in mind that if your dog is digging in your garden, it is quite normal behaviour.

Many ardent gardeners despair of their dog's constant digging. People often complain to me, 'As fast as I fill them in, he digs them out'. Just imagine for a moment that you have gone to a nursery, have bought a plant and brought it home. Next, you dig a hole to plant it in and go to fetch the plant, but when you return, you find someone has filled your hole in. What would you do? Would you go away or would you dig the hole again? Of course you would redig the hole. Your dog will do the same.

The most effective way to stop a dog from digging holes is to catch it in the act. To do this, you could deliberately bury something, such as food, and then hide and wait for your dog to dig it up. The moment your dog begins to dig, use your throw chain and say 'Bah', and keep repeating this until the dog stops digging.

Catching your dog in the act of digging is, however, very difficult. But, there are a few things you can try. After filling the holes your dog has dug, place some of the dog's droppings near the top; this should act as a deterrent to the dog digging there again. Another method is to place hot chilli powder in each hole your dog digs — first place some of it in your hand and let your dog get a good sniff of it so it will remember its unpleasantness.

These last two methods will prevent your dog from digging in certain places in the garden (those places where it has previously dug and are now booby-trapped), but they won't stop your dog from digging elsewhere. The best I can suggest is that you employ all three methods when trying to cure this particular behavioural problem.

PLANT AND GARDEN DESTRUCTION

Dogs do not know how much we treasure our plants and gardens. To a dog, the things growing in our gardens are just play things. Just as you would not leave a two-year-old child unattended in a china shop, you cannot expect a pup not to touch your plants if left to its own devices. A playpen is the best way of keeping a pup away from garden beds and young bushes. If you have a fully grown dog that likes gardening, try protecting your garden with a mesh fence, but this can prove expensive and not very attractive.

Fortunately, there are other methods you can use. Try putting pepper around the base of the plants, or scatter the dog's droppings in the garden beds and on top of treasured pot plants. You could also try catching your dog in the act (using the throw chain method and 'Bah') but never take a dog back to a decimated garden and punish it — it will be too late.

Get Off My Garden

A unique, very effective product available from most pet shops is called Get Off My Garden. It comes in green crystals which, when sprinkled on your garden, deter a dog from going near it for a long time. It is an Australian-made product, and is effective in all weather conditions.

Its repellent is suspended in the crystals, which are jelly-like when saturated with water. When it rains, they absorb more water and grow, but are not washed away. In hot weather, the crystals dry out, but the repellent stays 'locked in', to be released the next time it rains or the next time you water your garden.

The product is non-toxic and safe for your dog, but do read the instructions carefully and use as directed. It is available in Australia, New Zealand, America, the United Kingdom and most European countries, and retails for around $A10.

BARKING IN THE MIDDLE OF THE NIGHT

Dogs are naturally more protective at night, because in the wild this is when the pack was more vulnerable. Also, dogs mostly sleep during the heat of the day and become lively in the cool of the evening. So, just when you are at your least alert, your dog is at its most alert. The sounds of a normal day — traffic, pedestrians, factory sounds, and all the sorts of things that make up the suburban din which your dog becomes conditioned to — are nothing compared to the possums and cats that come out at night and get up to mischief. But since we need our sleep, the dog must be trained that barking at everything annoys us. Many people ask me, 'How can I be sure that if I stop my dog barking at possums and cats, it will still bark when someone is breaking into the house?' Well the answer is, you don't know for sure, but console yourself by remembering that dogs do possess a kind of 'sixth sense'.

CASE HISTORY: A Scottish collie named Sandy was a prolific barker. She barked at the broom, the vacuum cleaner, the lawn mower ... everything! With therapy, scene setting, and then follow-up therapy from the owners, Sandy was totally cured from barking at all. Some months after Sandy's cure her owner called to tell me that while he and his wife were in the house one day, they heard frantic barking coming from the pool area. They went outside to investigate and found their neighbours' two-year-old child sitting on the edge of the pool with Sandy standing nearby barking at him. The man who cleans the pool had inadvertently left the gate open. Sandy's owner said that if that had happened two months ago, they would not have gone out to investigate because the dog was always barking.

Though this experience happened during the day, the same applies at night. If your dog barks at everything that moves outside at night, it becomes like one of those car alarms that no one pays any attention to because they are always going off. So you will stop checking what your dog is barking at. The aim is to cure the dog of barking at all the nuisance things, but beyond this, its instinct should prevail when danger is around.

The cure for night barking, first of all depends on where your dog sleeps. If it sleeps in your bedroom, then it's easier

One way of training your dog to stop barking in the yard at night is to half fill several soft drink cans with pebbles and throw them at the ground or a fence as close as possible to the dog. This shock tactic, repeated several times, will teach the dog that barking will receive an instant reprimand.

for you to reprimand the dog. If your dog sleeps in the laundry, a downstairs area, or out in the yard, then it will be a little more difficult — you will have to resign yourself to a little more effort in the beginning, but eventually you will be able to reprimand the dog from your bed. (See also the section on barking at night in 'House Problems', page 93.)

To cure the dog that barks in the backyard at night, open a window near to where the dog usually barks. Have some missiles ready — either a couple of throw chains or several soft drink cans half-filled with pebbles — and throw them as close to the dog as possible or bounce them off the fence as soon as your dog starts barking. If your dog is nowhere near the house and it is impossible for you to reprimand it directly from any window, then you will have to set up an amplifier just outside a window by leaning a sheet of metal against the fence, for example, for the chain or can to hit. This method might wear thin with some very persistent barkers and you may find that you have to get up, go outside and throw the chain near your dog to reinforce the programming. Remember to yell 'Bah' when you throw the drink can or throw chain, and to praise your dog as soon as it behaves.

BARKING AT YOUR NEIGHBOUR

We all like to keep on friendly terms with our neighbours, and a dog that barks at them can cause disharmony. If your dog barks at your neighbours, ask them to help with the cure. Ask your neighbours to walk into their yard, and as soon as your dog starts to bark at them, you should reprimand it from your window by throwing your chain at the fence or near the dog's feet and say 'Bah'. (You can also fill plastic sandwich bags with water and throw them, aiming to hit your dog — they won't hurt; they will burst open on impact). Once you start the training session, you must keep reprimanding the dog every time it barks.

When your dog is responding reasonably well to the training, some scene setting will help to cure your dog much

To teach your dog not to bark at your neighbours, set the scene for a surprise reprimand. Hide in your neighbour's garden with your throw chain (a). As soon as your dog begins to bark at your neighbours, make an appearance and throw the chains as close as possible to the dog (b). Praise it when it stops barking.

faster. Pretend to go out, then sneak into your neighbour's yard and hide. Ask your neighbours to walk into their yard, and if your dog barks at them reprimand it with water bags or the throw chain. Praise your dog as soon as it stops barking. You could eventually allow the neighbours to reprimand your dog for you when you are out, providing the dog is not aggressive (see page 50 for further details on allowing someone else to reprimand your dog).

If you are not on good terms with your neighbours, then you may have to do it all yourself. Just wait for your dog to bark at the neighbours, then reprimand it as outlined above. You will have to be more patient under these circumstances; it will be impossible for you to fully co-ordinate the training and it will therefore take longer for you to cure your dog's barking problem, but do persevere. Always remember to praise your dog when it stops misbehaving.

BARKING WHILE YOU ARE IN THE POOL

You will need help to cure this habit because it is very hard to reprimand a dog while you are in the pool. The problem is made more difficult to cure because the splashing water excites the dog. Ask a member of the family to go for a swim while you hide nearby. As soon as your dog barks, jump out, use your throw chain and say 'Bah'. You might have to throw the chains a couple of dozen times until your dog stops barking. Do not stop until your dog does. When this happens, you might be able to reprimand your dog from the pool if the animal displays this behaviour again. (Reprimanding from the pool is not usually as effective because you lose authority over your pet when you are physically lower than it.)

It is not advisable to allow children to reprimand the dog as they lack the necessary dominance and the dog will only ignore their attempts.

Scene setting will prove very effective in gaining a faster cure with this problem. Organise some people to go for a swim, while you hide nearby. As soon as your dog barks at the swimmers, jump out to surprise it, throw the throw chain and say 'Bah'. Always remember to praise your dog the instant it stops misbehaving.

Pool Safety for Dogs and Pups

We have all heard horrifying stories of children drowning in backyard pools. We are all aware of the importance of pool safety where our children are concerned, but how many of us are aware of pool safety for animals, especially our dogs? Over the years I have heard many horrifying stories — which never reach the media — of dogs drowning in backyard pools. I have also heard many stories about people finding their dog in a distressed state because it had fallen or jumped into the pool and was unable to get out. One man I know returned home to find his dog close to collapse, hanging onto the side of the pool. The dog was unable to walk for a week. It had come very close to death.

If your dog or pup has access to your backyard pool, you should teach it pool safety. To do this, tie a long rope to a firm-fitting collar on your dog, then throw the dog into the pool. Pull on the rope and guide the dog to the pool steps. Make sure it can get out unaided. If it can't, then you might have to consider modifying the steps with some rubber strips or making a platform out of wood for the dog to climb onto if it accidentally falls into the pool. Keep putting your dog in the water and working with it until it automatically swims to the steps. You can then be confident that your dog will know where the steps are if it falls into the pool.

BARKING OR JUMPING AT THE BACK DOOR

Remember the rolled-up newspaper story I told you (page 30)? Well this is how you can cure that particular behavioural problem. As soon as the dog barks, instead of opening the door and hitting your dog with a newspaper, open a window near the back door and throw a water bag or throw chain, aiming near the dog, and saying 'Bah' at

If your dog jumps up at or barks through a flyscreen door, reprimand it by throwing your throw chain at the base of the door, saying 'Bah' as you do. Praise the dog when it behaves.

the same time. Repeat this procedure until the dog stops barking, then praise it.

To cure a dog that jumps up at the flyscreen or barks through it, a water sprayer works very effectively in most cases. Spray your dog through the screen as soon as it jumps or barks.

Dogs that jump up on glass sliding doors can be stopped by throwing the throw chain at the metallic base of the glass door. Be careful not to hit the glass as you might crack it. As soon as the dog stops its bad behaviour, let it know you are pleased with it by praising it.

BARKING WHEN A CAR COMES OR GOES FROM YOUR DRIVEWAY

What you need to do here is set the scene. Ask a friend to drive the car in or out of the driveway for you. Hide nearby, as close as you can without your dog seeing you.

When the dog starts barking, use the throw chain and the 'Bah' reprimand. Repeat the procedure several times until the dog stops reacting; when this happens, praise your dog.

BARKING WHEN YOU ARE OUT

To stop a dog barking when you are not at home you must set the scene. Pretend to go out, then sneak back and hide and have someone walk up and down the street with a dog. As soon as your dog barks, reprimand it by using the throw chain and saying 'Bah'. Arrange for different people and dogs to walk past, so that your dog doesn't think that it is just that particular person and dog it's not allowed to bark at. Praise your dog when it stops barking.

A method, which I have named the 'Duncan Method', can also be used to stop a dog barking when you are out. To explain the method I must first tell you how it all started.

CASE HISTORY: A German shepherd and a border collie cross both barked when their owner, Duncan, was out at work. Duncan received some complaints about the dogs, and so proceeded to find out what to do about their barking. He was first referred to a dog psychologist who told him to spend more time with the dogs and change their routine. Well, he couldn't spend any more time with them. As he had to go to work, the most he could manage was to walk his dogs morning and night. So he tried changing their routine, but the barking still continued.

It was then that Duncan made an appointment with Bark Busters and was shown the technique we use to cure this problem. He called me a few months later to say that the dogs were doing well; the barking had stopped when there was someone home but there were still some problems when everyone was out. I asked Duncan if a friendly neighbour could perhaps reprimand the dogs for him when he was at work, using the methods we had shown him. This, however, was too difficult because of the size of the properties and the distance the neighbour would have to travel to reprimand the dogs. For a short time, though, he had some success by taping his voice on a recording which could be activated when the phone rang so that a loud booming voice would yell 'Bah' over the air waves. All the neighbour then needed to do, was to ring the house every time he heard the dogs bark. Eventually, the dogs stopped barking the instant they heard the phone. It was an ingenious method, only it wore off.

Armed with the information that Duncan had given me, I devised a plan to programme the dogs to the phone once and for all. I told Duncan to ask someone to ring the house while Duncan hid on the other side of the fence. As soon as he heard the phone, he was to throw the throw chain as close to the dogs as possible and yell 'Bah'. I suggested he do this daily for one week, then reinforce it on a regular basis. In this way the dogs were completely cured. The neighbour only had to ring a few times and the dogs took it as a reprimand for barking.

I call this method the 'Duncan Method', as his ingenuity in trying to solve his problem developed a new technique. Now if people have this problem with their dogs, they just have to ask their neighbour to phone the house — and it won't even cost them the call as the dogs won't answer. Thanks Duncan.

BARKING WHILE PENNED OR CHAINED

I do not condone the chaining of a dog because I believe it is cruel. Mostly, dogs are chained because they are naughty and untrained. But, how anyone can keep a dog chained for long periods escapes me. It is far better to pen a dog than to chain it; at least it can walk around freely. On the other hand, I do realise some people have no alternative but to chain their dog — but if you do this, be sure to take it for walks and exercise it often.

Throw chains will cure the dog that barks while penned or chained, just bounce the chain off the dog's kennel and say 'Bah'. Praise your dog the instant it stops barking.

Do be sure to train your chained dog and give it plenty of attention. Legally, a chained dog should be given two hours' freedom in every 24 hours. If you do have a dog which you are afraid to let off the chain for one reason or another, do the dog a favour and build a pen and train it.

▶ CHAPTER SIX ◀

House Problems

In today's society, more and more dogs are found living inside their owner's house — with many people allowing them the complete run of the home. This means it is necessary to teach these dogs good house manners. Just as we prefer our children to be well behaved, it is quite reasonable to expect our dogs to behave when inside.

HOUSE MANNERS — AND HOW TO DEAL WITH THE BAD ONES

Good house manners, where a dog's concerned, simply mean calm behaviour. A dog that bounds about the house, knocks things flying, jumps all over the lounge, steals the cushions, and so on, is not behaving well.

If your dog is badly behaved when inside, an excellent way to start training is to teach it to move around calmly. Put the dog on a lead, letting it trail on the ground. As soon as the dog starts to bound around you can grab the end of the lead, giving it a yank, or stand on it, saying 'Bah'. This will show the dog that you are angered by its wild behaviour. Be sure to give your dog lots of time during these training sessions; it's not practical to try to cook dinner, while at the same time trying to watch everything the dog is doing. In the beginning, you will be saying 'Bah' rather a lot until the dog learns what it can and cannot do.

When you are confident that your dog can be controlled, take it off the lead and use your throw chain from then on to reinforce your 'Bah' reprimand. Remember to praise your dog when it stops misbehaving.

FOOD STEALING

A dog has no sense of right and wrong; it only knows what we teach it. Food left unattended is an open invitation. To stop a dog from stealing food, set the scene: place some food on a kitchen bench or a coffee table, then hide and wait for the dog to go for the food. Sneak up behind the dog and reprimand it by saying 'Bah' and using your throw chain. If catching the dog in the act proves too difficult, lace the food with something very hot and unpleasant tasting (like hot chilli). Either method works effectively.

Dogs that raid the kitchen garbage bin are a nuisance. A simple and effective cure is to spread a layer of plastic or newspaper over the rubbish and then liberally sprinkle cayenne pepper on top. Your dog will receive an unpleasant lesson as soon as it begins to rummage in the bin.

Raiding the Kitchen-tidy Bin

To cure this problem, set the dog up. Put your bin in a place where your dog can easily see it, and completely cover the rubbish with a piece of plastic or a piece of newspaper. Press the rubbish down so that the plastic or newspaper can sit flat. Cover the top of the paper or plastic with cayenne pepper, which will give the dog a bad experience when it next attempts to raid the bin. You could also bait some food and place it on top of the bin: shape some mince into a ball and place a bit of cayenne pepper right in the middle of it. It will quickly make your dog think that every food item that comes out of that bin is undesirable!

JUMPING ONTO THE BED OR LOUNGE

Jumping onto the bed or lounge is one of the more frequent habits I am asked to cure. It's not advisable to allow a little puppy to sleep with you in the belief that you will be able to stop the practice easily when the dog is fully grown. I know one lady who deeply regrets letting her dog develop this habit to this very day; she has an adult Great Dane that insists on sleeping with her every night because it was allowed to do so as a pup. She now doesn't have the heart to push the dog off the bed.

Many people have dogs that sneak into the bedroom while they are out or watching television. Though a common problem, it's quite easy to cure. First, set the scene: hide in the wardrobe, or under or behind the bed. Arm yourself with the throw chain, then be patient and very quiet. If your dog only jumps onto the bed when no one is there, you will have to wait for the dog to enter the bedroom and jump onto the bed. You should then jump out suddenly and throw the throw chain, saying 'Bah'. Praise your dog when it jumps down. There is an even simpler way, of course. Close your bedroom door. Nevertheless, training your dog not to jump onto the bed does make a lot of sense.

Set the scene to teach your dog not to jump on your bed. Hide in your wardrobe or behind your bed, and as soon as the dog leaps on to it, jump out and throw a chain, saying 'Bah'. Praise your dog when it jumps down.

The above method also works well in curing a dog that jumps onto the lounge. Just hide nearby and follow the steps given above. Another method is to throw the throw chain near the spot on the lounge your dog is heading for at the instant it begins to jump, saying 'Bah'. Again, praise your dog as soon as it jumps down.

JUMPING ON THE GUESTS

The quickest way to cure this problem is to arrange for some friends to visit you. Be ready with your throw chain, and as soon as your dog jumps up on them, throw it and say 'Bah'. Praise your dog the moment it stops jumping up. If you continually set the scene, you will train your dog much faster.

RUSHING THROUGH THE FRONT DOOR

Training is the same as that used for rushing through a gate or door in Yard Problems, page 66. Just adapt the procedures as necessary since the dog is now inside the house and wanting to rush out (for example, some things will be reversed, with you outside and the dog inside). You could also ask someone your dog knows and respects to hide outside and use the throw chain when you say 'Bah'. When your dog no longer rushes through the door, open the door and walk out, keeping your eye on the dog. If it attempts to follow you, say 'Bah' and throw the throw chain, aiming at the dog's feet. Progress to hiding outside yourself (with no one to check the dog at the door), and wait for your dog to venture through, then reprimand it.

Do not leave the door open for extended periods and expect the dog never to come through it, especially when you are not there. The object of the training is really only to stop the dog rushing through the front door each time you open it.

TOILET TRAINING

There are two clearly identifiable times that a pup or dog will need to relieve itself: one is as soon as it wakes up from a sleep; the other is directly after eating and drinking. If your dog lives inside your home, be sure to take it outside during these times. To house-train a young puppy, take it from its playpen and out to the garden several times during the day. Always take your pet to the same spot in the garden, and say 'Go to the toilet' over and over again. After a time the pup will know what you want it to do when it hears those words.

House-training a fully grown dog can be achieved by keeping it on a lead during these times and either tying it up or keeping it by your side. (Most dogs won't go to the toilet on-lead if they are used to normally being free — they won't want to soil the area near them.) Follow the same procedure as house-training a puppy. Under no

It's no good berating your dog after you have discovered it has made a mess in the house; the dog simply won't understand (a). Instead, toilet train the animal properly. As soon as it wakes up or has finished eating or drinking, take it to the same place in the garden and repeat the words 'Go to the toilet' until the animal does (b). Praise it. You will have to be consistent in this training but the dog will soon learn.

circumstances should you trust the dog to be left alone until you are sure good toilet habits have been adopted. Praise your dog each time it goes to the toilet in the right place, as this will encourage it to go there again.

Remember, you shouldn't punish the dog for fouling the house and *never* rub his nose in the mess. To do that would be like rubbing a baby's nose in its dirty nappy. Such accidents are not the dog's fault; a dog needs proper training if it is to do something right. Be patient, your dog will catch on in time.

ATTACKING YOUR CAT

Your pet cat and your pet dog *can* be taught to live in harmony. Stop your dog chasing your cat or showing aggression towards it and you will find your cat will eventually come to accept the dog. Begin by locking your dog and cat together in a room (this is to stop the cat disappearing as cats do). Put your dog on a lead and have your magic piece of equipment, the throw chain, ready. Concentrate on your dog. As soon as it becomes distracted by the cat, throw the chain at the dog's feet and say 'Bah'. Repeat this procedure until you start getting results. Some dogs will learn quickly; others will need repeated effort. Continue this training until your dog ignores your cat (about a week). It is not vital that your pets become friends, only that they learn to tolerate each other.

PESTERING YOU WHEN YOU ARE EATING

At mealtimes it is unwise to feed your dog titbits from the dinner table as this practice only encourages bad habits. A dog that is never fed in this way never anticipates it happening. Try to feed your dog at the same time you are eating your meals, then, if after it has eaten its meal it returns to pester you, reprimand it by saying 'Bah', and pointing away from the table to indicate you do not want it near the table at this time.

BARKING AT GUESTS

As mentioned earlier, dogs that bark at your guests are usually of a nervous disposition or conversely very dominant.

If your dog is the nervy type, set the scene. Ask a neighbour or friend to visit. Keep your dog on its lead to start with, and as soon as the dog barks, throw the chain near its feet and say 'Bah'. You will find it hard to stop dogs of this temperament from barking as their nervousness will overcome the fear of the reprimand. But persevere — nervous dogs are hard, but not impossible, to cure. If the chain accidentally hits the dog in this exercise, do not apologise to the dog as the chain will not hurt it; you must be tough with a nervous dog. Repeat the procedure several times, with different strangers coming to the door, until you totally desensitise your dog to other people. With a nervous dog, there is no need to make it friendly or allow the visitors to pat it; the dog only has to tolerate them without barking. Ask all future guests to ignore the dog and to make no attempt to pat it, this will calm it down. Confronting the dog puts pressure on it and causes unnecessary stress.

If you have a dominant, aggressive dog, you must employ a different technique. It will require two people that the dog knows and respects to effect a cure. (See section on allowing someone else to reprimand your dog, page 50.) Again, keep the dog on its lead. Ask a neighbour to act as a visitor and ask your helper to hide behind them. When you open the door, the helper should jump out from behind your visitor as soon as the dog barks, and throw the chain directly at the dog's feet saying 'Bah' in the most dominant voice they can summon up. If this isn't proving effective, then you and the helper will need a throw chain each so that both of you can reprimand the dog. Repeat this procedure until your dog stops barking, and then praise it. Do not attempt this off the lead until you are extremely sure the dog will not return to its bad habits. You will have to use several different 'strangers', otherwise the dog will only become desensitised to just one person.

Nervous dogs or dogs
with dominant
temperaments may bark
at visitors to your house.
If you have a nervous
dog and are expecting a
visitor, put the dog on a
lead. As soon as the dog
begins to bark, throw the
chain at its feet and
sternly say 'Bah'. Praise
the dog as soon as it
behaves.

Dogs with dominant
temperaments need a
different approach,
requiring three
participants. Again,
arrange for a visitor to
call and keep the dog on
a lead. Ask your helper to
hide behind the visitor
and as soon as the dog
barks when you open the
door, they should leap
out, throwing the throw
chain and saying 'Bah' in
the sternest voice they
can muster.

CASE HISTORY: A very aggressive Rottweiler had inexplicably become vicious towards some children who regularly visited its home. I was called in when the owners feared that they would have to put the dog down after it had attempted to attack the children. My plan of action was firstly to programme the dog, and then ask the children to enter the house. This was risky, but their parents insisted because they had discovered that the children had been tormenting the dog through the fence when no-one was home, and felt amends should be made. I placed the dog on its lead and arranged for the children to come in with the dog's owner hiding behind them. As soon as the dog became aggressive, the owner appeared from behind the children and reprimanded the dog with the throw chain and the word 'Bah'. We repeated this procedure until the dog behaved. The dog and the children can now be in the house together and the dog happily plays with them. The children have promised never to tease the dog again. The cure took only one visit from me and a week's follow-up by the owner.

BARKING IN THE MIDDLE OF THE NIGHT

If your dog sleeps in your bedroom, you can simply reprimand it with the throw chain and 'Bah' when it barks. However, if your dog sleeps downstairs, you will have to get out of bed, sneak down the stairs so that the dog cannot hear you coming, and catch it in the act of barking to reprimand it. When you have done this a couple of times, your dog will respect the throw chain, and you can then place a wok in your bedroom to amplify the sound and throw the chain into the wok whenever the dog barks.

You could also try using a metal receptacle (such as a colander), in conjunction with the throw chain. Anchor the chain to the top of the receptacle and allow the chain to hang into it. Hang the metal container near the dog, and attach some string to it so that when you pull the string in your room, the chain rattles in your dog's room. For this and the wok to work effectively, your dog must already respect the throw chain; in other words, you will initially have to get out of bed several times to reprimand your dog directly with the throw chain in order to make your point.

It can be dreary to have to get out of bed at night to reprimand your dog for barking in the house. You might have to do this using a throw chain a couple of times, but you will soon be able to stay in bed and simply throw the throw chain into a wok. This will amplify the sound and continue to reprimand the dog.

BARKING OUT OF THE WINDOW

Constant barking in the house can be very irritating for owners of over-protective dogs. If your dog is the type that barks as soon as it spots someone or something (a cat or another dog) walking past the house, it can turn you into a nervous wreck — not to mention what it can do to your neighbours. If you live in a unit, this type of behaviour could result in you having to move or even part with your over-exuberant pet.

Catch your dog when it's barking and use your throw chain and say 'Bah' to reprimand it. Give your dog a good experience by praising it the instant it stops barking. A particularly quick cure will result from scene setting. Ask a neighbour or friend to walk past the front of the house, maybe with a dog on a lead, and reprimand your dog whenever it barks. Do this several times or until the dog takes no notice of the passers-by. Always keep the throw chain handy for future outbreaks.

BARKING AT THE VACUUM CLEANER
AND THE BROOM

The vacuum cleaner must look and sound like a monster to your dog, who has no understanding of such things. Can you imagine what this evil-sounding thing must look like? No wonder so many dogs bark at them. Fortunately, it is an easy thing to cure. Keep your water sprayer or throw chain handy and use them in conjunction with 'Bah' to reprimand your dog the instant it starts barking at the vacuum. In the same way reprimand a dog that starts barking when you go to the cupboard where the vacuum is kept. Be prepared every time you are going to vacuum clean the carpet. Always praise your dog generously when it stops barking.

To cure a dog which barks at the broom, follow the same method used for the vacuum cleaner.

If your dog barks at the vacuum cleaner or broom, spray water in its face and say 'Bah' as soon as it barks. Praise the dog when it behaves. If your dog is not afraid of water, the throw chain is another effective method of reprimand.

▶ CHAPTER SEVEN ◀

Street and Farm Problems

In no way do I condone allowing a dog to roam the streets at will. During my years at the RSPCA, I saw too many dogs come to grief because their owners allowed them too much freedom. Many good dogs have been put down because they were run over and badly injured, attacked children or stock, or caused accidents by chasing cars. Remember, dogs do not have a conscience; they can very easily develop bad habits if left to their own devices.

Confining a dog to its yard is not necessarily cruel, despite what many people think. I always liken letting a dog run free in the street to letting a five-year-old child loose in a big city — think of all the horrible things that could happen to it. I know that many people let their dog out because it has either been destructive or too yappy. Rather than doing this, I strongly suggest that they train the dog to behave, and take it for walks on a regular basis.

Confining dogs on large properties or farms is sometimes difficult. Given the nature of farm dogs (their breeding and training have given them specific skills in handling stock), certain problems can arise when it comes to roaming about. This chapter looks at solving the street or farm problems you may be having with your dog.

AGGRESSION TOWARDS PEOPLE AND DOGS

A dog that shows aggression to anyone or anything while you are taking it for a walk must be strongly disciplined. If you are serious about curing this problem, you will have to let the dog know that you are *very* displeased with it. This type of behaviour usually stems from fear. Fear-aggression can be cured, but you must display very dominant behaviour; do not be shy when people are around, otherwise your dog is going to be condemned to a life locked away from everything. If showing aggression to your dog while strangers are watching embarrasses you, then ask some friends to help you by bringing a friendly dog with them so you can do some scene setting.

If using helpers, ask a couple of them to walk a dog down the street towards you. Have someone your dog knows and respects hide behind them. (See section on allowing someone else to reprimand your dog, page 50.) Walk your dog as close as possible to them with-in the limits of safety. As soon as your dog becomes aggressive, the person who is hiding should pop out and reprimand with 'Bah' and the throw chain. Your dog, not having an analytical mind, will start to think that your friend is always hiding behind anyone who walks down the street. Make sure you and the person who has been hiding pat the dog once it stops being aggressive.

Do not allow your dog to retreat. Many nervous dogs, once they have been cured of aggression, usually act as though retreat is the better part of valour and try to go in the opposite direction. If this does happen, say 'Bah', otherwise your dog may spend the rest of its life running away from strangers. By the same token, do not expect your dog to be friendly, especially if it has a nervous disposition.

If your dog has been effectively programmed, it should respond to this method relatively well. Alternatively, carry a chain yourself and reprimand by throwing the chain at the dog's feet and saying 'Bah'. For a very difficult dog, you could lift its front paws into the air for a few seconds each time it is aggressive. Reprimand your dog by saying

*If your dog barks or growls at people while out for a walk, one
method to teach it to behave is to jerk the dog off its front paws for
a couple of seconds, saying 'Bah' as aggressively as you can. Repeated
a few times, with praise for good behaviour, this technique will soon
teach a dog to ignore strangers.*

'Bah' if it growls, even slightly, as this is often a warning
signal that the dog is going to bark. Also you should not
let someone your dog does not know reprimand it because
this will only make the dog more aggressive to strangers.

If, when walking your dog, you are confronted by an
aggressive dog that comes running out at you, do not stop,
keep walking. Stopping will only allow the dogs to confront
each other and maybe even fight. Keep your concentration
on your dog; keep your dog heeling and reprimand it if it
refuses to obey you and ignore the other dog. The throw
chain can also be used to keep aggressive dogs at bay. A
throw chain attached to a long light lead may come in
handy on your walks. You can throw it at an aggressive
dog's feet — not to hit it, just to startle it. It won't work

on all dogs because a dog usually needs to be programmed before it will respond. However, I have found this does work on a high percentage of dogs.

TIMIDNESS TOWARDS PEOPLE AND DOGS

Very timid dogs will try anything to avoid confrontation with people and other dogs. Make sure your dog is programmed and obedient to you in the yard before you venture out. As explained in the section on temperament, you need to be tough with nervous dogs. They require your help, not your pity. To pity your dog will only allow it to remain scared out of its wits. I have trained many terrified dogs to walk successfully past strangers and other animals — the trick is to make the dog more fearful of getting into trouble from me than worrying about the strangers. Once your dog realises the object of its fear won't hurt it, it will walk by calmly on a loose lead. Praise your dog when it is behaving well.

The best way to get quick results is once again to set the scene. Ask a couple of people to walk towards you in the street, while you hold the lead loosely and keep your dog heeling, snapping the lead and saying 'Bah' every time your dog tries to move out of position. Request the helpers to walk up and down the street several times until your dog no longer worries about them. Be sure to use different people over a period of several days. If your dog starts to react badly, do not stop. Be tough! Your perseverance will pay dividends. Your dog should eventually walk on your left side, on a slack lead, without reacting to strange encounters.

PULLING ON THE LEAD

As I've explained elsewhere, pulling is a natural thing for a dog to do, but it can be very disconcerting for the dog's owner! A dog will pull on its lead all day unless it is trained to do otherwise. Many people tell me that they have stopped walking their dog because it would forcefully pull them along the street, embarrassing them. Having cured hundreds of dogs of this habit, I find that the owners all made the same mistake: they would wrap the lead firmly around their hands and hang on for grim death. They would also keep the lead as short as possible, and usually walk the dog using a leather collar and sometimes even a chain lead. A dog should always be walked on a very loose lead; and the longer and softer the lead the better; a soft webbing lead 2 metres (6 feet) long is recommended. A check chain is also required during training.

If your dog is a wild puller, the next time you take it for a walk, stop the walk every time your dog goes to the end of the lead, snap the lead and say 'Bah'.

Continue in this fashion until your dog realises that each time it gets to the end of the lead, it will be checked. The correct technique is as follows: when your dog is pulling tightly on the lead, step forward to give the lead slack and then snap it back sharply, taking a couple of steps back. Do this quickly, otherwise the dog will race ahead. Try to keep your dog's front legs in line with your legs. Praise your dog when it is in the correct position. (Don't forget that your dog has spent years at the end of its lead and thinks that is where it should be. Your pet does not know any better. Remember it takes technique to control a dog, not strength. I am only 155 centimetres (5 feet) tall, and I can control Great Danes and Rottweilers that are a lot stronger than me.)

If you find it difficult to master this technique, there is a very handy training aid called a 'Halti' which works in the same way as a halter on a horse by controlling the dog's head, thus giving you more control. The dog cannot pull like it can with a collar or check chain. The Halti also proves very advantageous with an aggressive dog, as the more the dog pulls, the more the Halti closes firmly on the dog's mouth, releasing the instant the pulling stops. I know many people who walk some very strong dogs beautifully at heel on a Halti. Haltis are available in all sizes from veterinary clinics and pet shops.

Too many people walk their dogs on a tight lead, which must be very uncomfortable for both owner and dog. But, pulling is a problem that can be cured. I recommend that you try the Bark Busters technique first and then, if it does not meet with success, try the Halti.

GOING TO THE VET

Many dogs fear going to the vet, especially if the only time a dog travels in the car is when it goes to the clinic. If the only time a dog goes to the vet is to receive a needle, then the journey becomes associated with pain and trauma.

Since a very important part of your dog's life is its regular visits to the vet (your dog will need regular checkups, immunisations and worming treatments to stay healthy), you must ensure there is no fear involved in getting your dog there. Always take a treat with you and ask the vet

Visiting the vet can be a frightening experience for your dog. Take treats and ask the vet to give the dog one; hold the dog's head and make a fuss of it. If it behaves aggressively, reprimand it immediately.

to give it to your dog, so your dog will associate good things with the visit. Always pat your dog profusely when it's receiving an injection; holding its head and patting will help take its mind off the needle. Reprimanding your pet severely for any aggression will help prevent it from happening again. An extremely aggressive dog may need to be muzzled, but if you're dominant enough, your dog should stop any silly behaviour.

A good way to make visits to the vet less traumatic for your dog is to take it with you when you are just going to the clinic to buy something. Sit in the waiting room, give your dog its treat, buy what you need and leave. This helps socialise the dog and alleviate its fear of the clinic.

If your dog is still young and not fully immunised, do not place it on the ground at the vet's or any place else as it could easily catch a disease. Carry it in your arms. I often see people allowing little puppies to trail along behind them in the streets. These owners are risking their pup's health as they could very easily pick up distemper or parvo virus. Contact your local vet for information on the correct immunisation for your dog or pup.

JUMPING AROUND IN THE CAR

A dog that jumps around in the car can be distracting for the driver and can even cause an accident. It is a very common problem with dogs, but one which can be easily cured.

Ensure your dog's collar fits firmly, then tie two leads to the collar and attach the ends of the leads to either side of the car. This will secure your dog to one area of the car, your dog's movements will be restricted, and good car travelling manners will be promoted. The leads can be removed once your dog understands that you want it to sit still. This may take months, but persevere and you'll get results.

If you have a puppy that jumps around in the car, hook the leads high so that the pup doesn't get tangled up in them; you can do this by closing the windows on the leads to secure them. Be sure to give enough slack to your pup or dog so that it can lie down comfortably.

It's a good idea to introduce a dog to car travel while it is still very young, since good car travelling manners are more easily learnt early in life — and it's far easier to control a pup than a fully grown dog if it's being naughty.

BARKING IN THE CAR

This habit can be cured in a number of ways, depending on your dog's temperament. Enlist a member of the family or a friend to help you (see page 50 for further details on allowing someone else to reprimand your dog). Attach two leads to your dog's collar and tie each lead to either side of the car so that the passenger (your helper) can easily reprimand it. You will need the water sprayer, the wok and the throw chain. If your dog hates water, try the water sprayer first. As soon as your dog starts to bark have the helper squirt the dog in the face with the water and say 'Bah'. He or she will need to do this several times until the dog catches on that every time it barks it gets squirted in the face.

Another method is to place a wok on the floor in the back-seat section of the car then ask your helper to throw the throw chain into it and say 'Bah' whenever the dog barks. Again, repeat this several times until your pet catches on. Or, your helper can throw the chain at the dog's feet, and say 'Bah'.

If none of these methods prove successful, you will need to remove the dog from the car and apply the strong reprimand training technique outlined on page 49. Then return to the car and try using the throw chain again. There are very few dogs that need the strong reprimand treatment, as most respond fairly quickly to the basic methods.

Barking in the car may prove more difficult to cure than other barking because when you are sitting down in the car, you lose a lot of the authority of height. However, if a dog has already been cured of barking in the backyard,

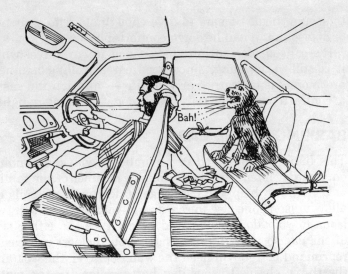

Many dogs become excited by car travel. To stop your pet from
leaping around, attach it securely to the doors using two leads (one to
each door). If your dog barks when it is in the car, keep a wok on the
floor and throw the chain into it, yelling 'Bah', until it stops. Praise
the dog as soon as it behaves.

for example, it is then at least familiar with the reprimand
procedure and will respond fairly quickly. Remember to
praise your dog the instant it begins to behave.

BARKING IN THE BACK OF A UTILITY

Quite a number of dog owners with utilities have this
problem. It is definitely one of the harder habits to break
because of the dog's location outside the cabin of the
vehicle, that is, separated from you. Although it's not easy
it can be done; I have cured dozens of dogs using the
following procedure.

You will need a friend to help you (see 'Asking Other
People to Reprimand Your Dog', page 50) and a secluded
road with very little traffic. The first couple of times your
dog barks, stop the truck, jump out and reprimand it with

the throw chain and say 'Bah'. As your dog could have stopped barking by this time, it may sound contradictory to reprimand it then (that is, not when it is in the act of misbehaving). But what you need to do here is give your dog some respect for the chain first, otherwise the next step in the procedure won't work.

Now, ask your helper to drive the ute while you hide near the road at some point along the route the vehicle will take. Then, when it passes that point and your dog is barking, jump out, yell 'Bah' and throw the throw chain into the tray. It's best if your helper doesn't drive too fast during this procedure.

Repeat this several times until your dog is quiet. You may need to repeat the procedure in different locations, so that your dog doesn't associate the reprimand with just one spot. If you have done the initial training properly, it will not take too many throws to completely cure the dog. It might only be necessary for you to get out and reprimand your dog in each new situation to re-establish your authority. Praise your dog when it stops barking.

BARKING WHEN LEFT ALONE IN THE CAR

Take your dog for a drive to a very secluded area; this will make it far less embarrassing for you when you reprimand your dog. Select the area carefully. It must be somewhere where you can disappear behind a tree, and then sneak up on the car without your pet seeing you. In the initial stages of training, it is a good idea to tie up your dog. That way you can leave a window open through which to reprimand it.

So, pretend to leave your dog tied up in the car, then sneak back without it seeing you. When it starts to bark, surprise it and throw the throw chain in through the window to land near your dog and say 'Bah'. Praise your dog when it stops barking.

Once you have done this several times and your dog is beginning to respond, enlist a member of the family or a friend to reprimand the dog for you as you are walking away. You will need to do this for about a week. Make sure that you reprimand your pet no matter what the situation. If you have done enough training in secluded areas, it won't take much to stop the dog's bad behaviour elsewhere.

CHASING MOTORCYCLES AND CARS

Dogs that chase bikes and cars can be a real danger to themselves as well as to the person driving the vehicle. To break this dreadful habit, you will need a bucket of water and two helpers: one to drive the car (or ride the bike) and one to let the dog into the front yard after you have hidden nearby. Dogs usually follow the same path when they chase cars, so establish the path your dog takes and hide along that line.

As soon as your dog begins to chase the car, appear in the animal's path, throw the bucket of water over it and

Car chasing is a dangerous habit — not only for your dog but for motorists, too. Training a dog will require three people: a driver, a person to let the dog into the front yard after you have hidden nearby, and you. Keep a bucket of water ready and as soon as your dog runs after the car, appear in the dog's path, throw the water over the dog and yell 'Bah'. Car chasing is a hard habit to break, so the training may have to be repeated several times.

yell 'Bah'. In this way your dog receives the reprimand while it's in full flight. It's best to have a driver who is aware of what will happen help you with this training. A barking, chasing dog, and a person throwing a bucket of water at it and yelling 'Bah' could easily distract an unknowing driver and be dangerous. And, of course, it is best to carry out this training during the quiet times on your street when traffic is minimal.

Instead of using a bucket of water, you can use your throw chain to reprimand the dog. However, this method does have its shortcomings: the noise of the car or bike can drown the sound of the chain, lessening its effectiveness. But persevere, and employ the strong-reprimand technique (page 49) if necessary.

Car chasing is a difficult problem to cure. You will need to repeat this training with several different cars, or motorcycles, before you can be sure that your dog is completely cured. Otherwise, your dog may only relate the reprimand to the particular vehicle used. It will take several days of concentrated effort to cure this problem. If after that time, you are still not having success with your pet, you might have to seek expert help.

CASE HISTORY: A trail bike enthusiast bought a 12-month-old male border collie to take trail riding with him. Unfortunately, the animal developed such a bad habit of attacking the wheels of the bike, that the man had accidentally ran over the dog a couple of times, requiring a trip to the vet. None of this, however, deterred the dog from chasing the bike and attacking its wheels. This dog was not going to give up its bad habit easily, so I was called in.

I programmed the dog, then asked the owner to get his trail bike out. Unfortunately, every time I jumped into the dog's path with the throw chain when it was chasing the bike, it would bark aggressively at me. Even though I had programmed the dog initially to gain its respect, it was clear that it had a very dominant temperament and wasn't going to take orders from a stranger.

So I asked the owner to throw the throw chain while riding his bike. The dog responded immediately and stopped barking. We

continued the training until finally the dog would sit quietly while
the owner rode his bike up and down the property.

FEAR OF TRAFFIC

A most effective way to get your dog used to traffic is to
take it to the busiest street in town, find a seat and sit
down and read a book. This way the dog will eventually
realise that the traffic won't hurt it. The mounted police
train their horses in much the same way, since a police
horse has to be used to traffic. Anyone who has seen a
mounted policeman controlling traffic and crowds will
realise that nothing seems to distract the horse. This is
because the horse has been completely desensitised to all
noises, traffic sounds and shocks. In the same way, you
can desensitise your dog by giving it a wide experience of
people and traffic. Sit calmly with your dog in this manner
for a week, then attempt to walk it up and down the street.
Keep the lead loose, and reprimand your dog if it reacts
badly to trucks and cars. Praise your dog when it stops
reacting badly to the traffic.

STOCK CHASING

A Puppy that Chases Stock

The best time to get a dog used to stock (for example, horses,
goats, cattle and sheep), is when it is a puppy. It is much
easier to stop a pup chasing stock than it is to stop a fully
grown dog in mid flight.

On a long, light lead (venetian blind cord or mower cord
approximately 6 metres [20 feet] long) take the pup towards
the stock. If your pup shows any aggression or is inclined
to want to chase the stock, give it a strong reprimand by
tugging the lead firmly and saying 'Bah' very sternly.
Remember to praise it when it behaves. With regular visits
to the stock, your pup will soon learn that it is not allowed

to chase them. Do not let your pup near stock unsupervised until you are confident that it will behave properly.

A Fully Grown Dog that Chases Stock

If you have a grown dog that chases stock, or have inherited a dog with that problem, here is a cure you can use.

Your dog must be programmed before you begin. Take it near the stock on a long, light lead, and carry your throw chain with you. Stir up the stock by chasing them yourself. Stay in control, wait for the dog to join in, then stop in

Chasing stock is a very bad habit: in fact, not only can it exhaust stock, but your dog runs the risk of being shot by an angry stock owner. First put your dog on the long lead, then stir up the herd slightly so that your dog is tempted to chase it. Brace yourself in case the dog runs to the end of the lead. Throw the throw chain near the dog's feet and yell 'Bah'. Praise it when it stops running. In time you will be able to let the lead trail on the ground and, finally, let the dog off the lead. But be ready with the throw chain in case the dog still has not quite learned its lesson.

your tracks and brace yourself in case the dog runs to the end of the lead, yell the reprimand 'Bah', and throw the chain, aiming near your dog's hind legs. Praise your dog when it behaves. If your dog refuses to stop, you will have to employ the strong-reprimand training (page 49) before you next attempt to cure your dog. The strong-reprimand technique is particularly useful here, as quite often when the throw chain is used in a paddock or in the backyard, it lands on grass, which muffles the sound. For this reason your dog might show no respect for the chain. When you have completed the strong-reprimand technique, return your dog to the stock area and start again.

Once your dog responds to training and realises that you do not want it to chase the stock, you could eventually allow the lead to trail on the ground. In time you will be able to allow the dog off the lead and just use the voice reprimand whenever it misbehaves. This takes time, so be patient.

Before you leave your dog unattended around stock, try the following method: Hide near the stock, and enlist someone to let your dog out as soon as you are in place. When your dog starts moving quickly towards the stock, jump out, throw the chain and say 'Bah'. If your dog is caught on enough occasions and not allowed near the area between training times, it will think you are always guarding the stock. Praise your dog the instant it behaves.

This method will have to be used on all the different stock situations you have on your property. For example, if you have a flock of sheep, a few cattle and a number of horses, you will need to train the dog with each type of stock you have in order to achieve a complete cure. If you only train your dog with horses, then the dog will only associate the reprimand with horses and is likely to continue chasing other varieties of stock.

BAILING PEOPLE UP

To cure this habit, scene setting is important — and you will need brave helpers. First, tie your dog up near the front of the house or wherever the dog normally bails people up. Ask someone the dog knows to distract it while you leave the property armed with your throw chain. Re-enter the property, without the dog seeing you, and hide behind the helpers as they walk into the area. As soon as the dog barks, appear from behind them, throw your chain and say 'Bah'. Praise your dog the instant it behaves. Repeat this procedure several times until your dog stops being aggressive. Then try the procedure with the dog roaming free.

Be diligent between training sessions. If someone enters the property and you are not expecting them, your dog could have them bailed up before you realise it. This makes breaking the habit that much more difficult because obviously you will not always be hiding behind your visitors, and the dog is likely to escape without a reprimand. With this in mind, it is safest to tie the dog up between the training sessions; this will ensure a quicker cure. If tying your dog up is not possible, yell 'Bah' or throw the chain through a window when you see people approaching; your dog must be made to realise that you do not condone its behaviour. You must be tough and overcome your dog's aggression. You will need to repeat this procedure with different strangers but you will find it easier to control the dog after a couple of good responses — your dog will start to think that you are behind every stranger that comes to the property.

Call to unsuspecting visitors to stand totally still. In this way they can avoid being bitten when the dog charges at them. Nevertheless, a dog that attacks people can cause trouble for you and it is against the law to keep a savage dog.

KEY POINTS

- *Never* tolerate aggressive behaviour from your dog towards yourself or anyone else. Always reprimand your dog the instant it shows any aggression.

- *Always* supervise dogs and children when they are together.

- If you ever allow someone else to reprimand your dog, make sure the dog has respect for that person. It may be necessary for the other person to carry out some programming with your dog before they attempt to reprimand it.

- Specific problems need individual attention — but whatever problem your dog has, the techniques in this book (scene setting, the throw chain and the water method) can be applied to achieve results.

- With correct programming and training, the word 'Bah' can eventually be used on its own to stop your dog from doing something you do not want it to do.

- Training must be done for five minutes a day, every day, in order for you to maintain dominance over your dog and for your programming to remain effective. Just work through some sit-stay, drop-stay, and gate and door training techniques.

▶ CONCLUSION ◀

Your dog is a pack animal and lives by pack law. Just as the more subordinate dogs in a pack will sometimes challenge the pack leader, expect your dog to challenge your leadership on a regular basis. Your dog is just testing you to be sure you are still capable of leading. These challenges may only be minor, but it is vital that you are consistent in your leadership — only in this way will your dog continue to respect you.

Keep in mind that you are your dog's protector and its teacher — its behaviour depends entirely on you. If you ignore what your dog is doing, or if your reprimand is ineffective, it will seem as if you are condoning its actions. If your dog should prove too difficult for you to deal with, seek professional help. If all your best efforts (and those of others) fail, then your local RSPCA or Animal Welfare organisation may be able to relocate your dog for you.

When thinking about problem dogs and their long-suffering owners, I remember a breeding kennel I once visited, owned by Stuart and Wendye Slatyer (breeders of champion Afghans and whippets). They have over 40 dogs in their care, each one immaculately groomed, but the thing that stands out in my mind is the complete control they had over each dog. When the dogs were loose in the yard, Stuart could simply open each kennel, call each dog by name, and one by one they would go into their respective kennels without any resistance. There was no doubt who the pack leader was. Nor would you ever find happier dogs than these. So keep this in mind: if Wendye and Stuart can manage 40 dogs, then there is a lot of hope for you and your dog or dogs.

If you discipline, educate, feed, shelter and generally look after your pet, and if you establish and maintain your role as leader, then it will repay you with respect, love and devotion. You will soon see that a well-behaved dog is a happy dog and a potential best friend. Dogs do not ask much for the services they provide: they can be our protectors or companions (I know many lonely or elderly people who would be lost without their dog); they can lead the blind, help track people lost in the bush, or find people buried by avalanches and earthquakes; they can herd stock, apprehend criminals, and much, much more.

As dogs owners we must ensure that the dog's reputation is well protected. By training our dogs and by being responsible owners, dogs would be more readily accepted into our society as there would be fewer horrifying headlines which malign our four-legged friends. But we can only do this by having a complete understanding of what makes the dog tick, and then by setting out to train and educate any dog in our care. Surely we can do that much: one of the most favourite animals in the world deserves the best we can give it.

▶ APPENDIX ◀

THE CORRECT ENCLOSURE, KENNEL AND CHAIN

If you find it necessary to confine your dog in any way, you should ensure that it is well provided for. A good pen size is approximately 4 metres (13 feet) by 3 metres (10 feet) if your yard size allows it. The sleeping quarters should face north and the entry gate should be close to this. This is because a dog will always go as far away as possible from its bed to relieve itself; if the gate is at the opposite end to the sleeping quarters, the dog will be going to the toilet right near the entrance. I know it is probably too expensive for existing kennels to be restructured to take this into account, but if you are building a new pen, please follow this advice. Water and food bowls should also be kept very close to the sleeping quarters, as dogs do not like to relieve themselves near their eating dishes.

Make sure the dog's kennel or sleeping box is large enough for your particular breed of dog, but not so large as to lose warmth. A kennel that is too big will allow too much cool air to circulate and will be cold in winter. Hessian is a very suitable bedding material. Padded hessian mats are available from most pet shops.

If you need to put your dog on a chain, the only suitable one, as far as I am concerned, is a running chain. The chain is hooked to a running wire, which in turn is anchored between two trees or posts, or from the dog's kennel to a post, with a stop so the dog cannot wrap itself around the post or tree. These running wires are available from most pet shops. This type of chain provides a lot more freedom of movement for the dog than standard chains. It also allows the dog to relieve itself a reasonable distance from its sleeping quarters.

▶ INDEX ◀